SNIDELINES:
TALKING TRASH
TO POWER

"Susie Day is precisely not part of a trend. Whether interviewing a Jesus weary of his own brand, promoting Santa Claus to NSA chief, or bringing us into the experiences of those she cherishes, her hilarious deadpan wire reports and heart on-the-sleeve homages form a category unto themselves. These are humane bulletins from a dehumanizing time, where the news is that laughter, tears, and commitment still matter."

— *Mark Sullivan, author of* **Slag: Poems**

SNIDELINES:
TALKING TRASH TO POWER

"It's precisely because Susie Day is writing
from the barricades that these caustic fables
and topsy-turvy news items are so hilariously,
debilitatingly funny. There's no ironic distance
here, but a lucid clarity that exposes the
ludicrous roots of business as usual."
— *Alison Bechdel, cartoonist*

"Susie Day's insistent voice provides us
not only with clarity about some of the most
vexing issues we face, but with signature
humor that keeps us from breaking beneath
the weight of the inhumanity and inequities
she documents. This collection of essays
should be required reading for all."
— *asha bandele, author,* **The Prisoner's Wife**

"What if Thomas Paine had been funnier?
Or Fran Lebowitz was leftier?
Read S*nidelines: Talking Trash to Power* and
let the trash-talking revolution start!"
— *Laura Flanders, author and
broadcast journalist, host of* **GritTV**

SNIDELINES: TALKING TRASH TO POWER

BY SUSIE DAY

ABINGDON SQUARE PUBLISHING
New York

SNIDELINES:
TALKING TRASH TO POWER
is published by
Abingdon Square Publishing Ltd.
463 West Street, Suite G122
New York, NY 10014
www.abingdonsquarepublishing.com

Design: Abingdon Square Publishing
Illustrations © 2014 by Maria Pia Marrella

ISBN 978-0-9830762-5-4
Library of Congress Control Number: 2014948376

First printing: November 2014
Printed in the United States of America

For Laura Whitehorn

TABLE OF CONTENTS

PART 2: A COUPLE OF CLOSE-UPS

INTRODUCTION

Quick! Before the next terrible thing happens, read this book. Before the next nuclear meltdown, the next terrorist attack—before radioactive seawater from melting glaciers pours into your living room and washes away your collection of Hummel figurines—before a meteor crashes into your hope chest and the villain in the black cape and mustache forecloses on your ranch, read this book. Read this book before the next good-looking psychopath becomes the next President of the United States—before the National Security Agency enters into a corporate merger with the Hulk, and Jesus comes back as Godzilla—before you stop caring about . . . whatever it was that was more important to you than anything else.

This book will not prevent or stop bigotry, climate change, federal surveillance, corporate plunder, or disasters, both natural and unnatural. But it could educate you as to the elite depravity of ultra-left PC thugs, such as myself, should Fox News ever call you for an interview.

Warning: Sometimes there aren't a lot of laughs, here. That's because most of the pieces in this book are satire. And, while people associate satire with laugh-out-loud funny, anybody who's read Jonathan Swift's "A Modest Proposal" knows that satire needn't have a lot of yuk-yuk. After all, the prospect of the Irish selling their babies as meat in order to climb out of poverty isn't exactly knee slapping. What matters is that satire points out an absurd amount of amorality ironically embedded in everyday life.

Speaking of infant-eating, how about those wacky United States? Although this country was founded on the principle that real Americans don't eat babies, it does spend trillions of dollars to bomb selected countries and blow apart the small, unselected bodies of infants and children. Right there, you could point to several embedded ironies, one being the fact that this government—undaunted by any other on the planet—regularly caves to the forces of Pro-Life, which have all but gutted access to government-funded abortion. Not real funny, but grounds for satire.

The pieces collected here have appeared, over the last twenty or so years, as columns in actual and virtual publications such as *Gay Community News, Z Magazine, Outweek, Sojourner, Windy City Times, Gay City News, SleptOn, Seven Oaks, Truthout,* and *MRzine.* Some of these are still going; many have folded over the years. All the real-life statistics, facts, events, and quotations in my essays have been checked and verified, because, even though some of my story lines may be outlandish, the truth still matters. Although I haven't provided the mountains of footnotes that I could have, there are a few endnotes for some of these pieces.

I wrote these satires and small essays from the snidelines of my multi-layered, many-splendored, irony-fortified life. I wrote for leftist or queer or lefty queer communities where I've lived. They're still alive, and so am I, and so, for that matter, are you, and I think we can all agree these are good things. So you should read this book before you die.

One more thing. I wear a hat. There's a series of hat drawings going on here. The first piece might explain something about the hat.

New York City, Bastille Day, 2014

PART I:
SOME
WIDE-ANGLE
SHOTS

STREET LIFE
OF A
MAD-HAT
ACTIVIST

Hey, what's up, lady? You got a problem with my hat? I mean, I was just walking down the street, minding my own business on my way to the A train, and you, an ordinary, middle-aged white lady in a blue plaid housedress, stop to glare at my hat. How friendly is that?

This is a good hat, lady, a cool hat. My girlfriend got it for me. Yeah, my luv-muffin lesbo girlfriend, see? She got me this tough, proletarian, newsboy's cap. Says to the world, "I may be cute, but I'm still a dyke." You got a problem with that? You don't like that I am wearing a homo hat?

Oh, I see I'm scaring your little pug dog, *yap, yap, yap*. So what? Maybe little puggie here is afraid I'll sweep you into my arms and rain ardent kisses upon your upturned, horrified face. What do you say, pug? Or would you prefer that we got married first?

I'm sure you've heard that homosexuality is not a disease, lady. We queers may be going to hell, but we're going there with a certificate of mental health from the American Psychiatric Association. For what that may be worth. I shower, I shave, I'm symmetrical. There's nothing wrong with me, other than the fact that you don't like my hat.

It's too "mannish," isn't it, lady? Too "unfeminine"? My hat subtly tells you that, if my girlfriend and I were to get married, I would be the groom. That the night before, there would be a stag party with whips and spike heels and hairy, tattooed bulldykes throwing their femmes over Harley-Davidsons—and everybody would be wearing these hats. Isn't that what you think, lady? Oh, SHUT UP, little puggie.

All I'm doing is wearing this hat, lady. Big, big so-what deal. But I can see you hate my hat. Hat hatred is a terrible thing. So many hats suffer needlessly. Compared to indiscriminate drone strikes, my hat, for you, is real pain. I'm trying to empathize, here, lady, how'm I doing?

It's hard being a lady in a blue plaid housedress, with no hat and a yappy dog, isn't it? There are no blue plaid Pride Marches for your kind, no special

bookstores, no blue-plaid-pug-dog issues to defend on MSNBC. You face ever-increasing food prices, your health care won't pay for your mammograms, and you carry, deep within your subconscious, the chronic awareness that the Indian Point nuclear power plant supplying our city's energy could, any day, send out radioactive plumes that would kill us all within a week. Yet you, for some reason, decide to fixate your existential malaise on my hat.

I suppose, because you are relatively powerless, I enjoy venting on you. I should be grateful that you are not a gang of white frat jocks who would do more than merely sneer at my hat. And I admit that, while I sort of like your housedress, I do see you as a stereotype. It's hard for me not to think of you as "one of them." Because I am so sick of all the snide little glances "you people" give off when "we" pass.

But I have a large soul. I can forgive. I forgive you, lady. My hat gives me this power.

So, if you have a problem with my hat, if my choice of chapeau oppresses you, please tell me. Go for it, lady. Share. It will bring peace.

Our time on this planet is limited and shortens, even as you glare. And yet, would your life improve if I actually took off my demented Sapphic headgear? I think not. That's the whole point, isn't it?

I can't explain it, but your life, would, in fact, be somehow diminished if I, to make you happy, removed this hat. And so I shall wear my hat—for you, lady. I shall wear my hat as I walk past you and your yappy dog.

For you, I shall wear this hat as I ride the A train downtown to stridently protest the latest U.S.-sponsored war. Perhaps I will not be taken seriously because of my hat. Perhaps the U.S. will continue sponsoring wars—but that will not be the fault of my hat.

So I shall wear this hat, lady. I shall wear it in the wind and the rain and in police wagons and on sunny days at the beach. And someday, lady, someday—I shall maybe even wear this hat as I grant you asylum on my newly liberated, strife-free island, soon after the Revolution.

MIRACLE ON PENNSYLVANIA AVENUE:

SANTA CONFIRMED AS NSA HEAD

WASHINGTON – After a brief debate, the Senate voted 98-0 today to confirm Santa Claus, bag-toting icon of festive home invasions, for a lifetime term as director of the NSA. Upon learning of the decision, Mr. Claus let out a triumphant "HO HO HO," shook his ample red belly, and handed out gaily wrapped iPhones to all, senator and page alike.

Santa's appointment, along with the ouster of the current NSA chief, is hoped to dispel rampant accusations that the National Security Agency has abused its power by spying on civilians.

"It's good that Santa's at the reins," said the President. "He makes national surveillance so heartwarming. Hey, what say we get Santa to take the fall for hounding Edward Snowden?"

During a half-hour confirmation hearing, Santa explained that, as an embodiment of Western culture's bounty, with magic powers to look into the hearts of every human being, he needs no permission to monitor email, phone calls, or financial records. Simply by riding around in his sleigh, says Santa, he can circumvent the courts in a way previous administrations could only dream of doing.

"The guy's an investigative genius," stated the Senate Select Committee on Intelligence Chairperson, reflecting bipartisan approval. "He's also a pagan symbol, so the church-state-separation loonies can't hammer us. Plus, Santa's so darn likeable, who could resist him? And he gives such good stuff. Look, my iPhone has an app that emits mild electrical shocks when you say something idiotic—OW!"

But Santa has a master plan, caution the anonymous "Santa's Helpers," who are concerned about a possible return to McCarthyism. In order to cut through surveillance red tape, they warn, Santa is creating one all-encompassing List, designating everyone as either "Naughty" or "Nice." There are, say the Helpers, no legal safeguards to ensure that the List will be checked once, let alone twice.

Telephone companies, Internet service providers, banks, and social networks have sometimes voiced reluctance to surrender client information to the government. Now, in hopes of making the "Nice" list, most appear eager to be shaken down by a merry fat man. Reactions of ordinary Americans, however, are mixed.

Clyde Lichtenloafer, sequin placement manager for the Ice Capades, said he was delighted by Santa's appointment, which makes the routine invasions of his private life more appealing. "Now, whenever I pick up the phone," said Mr. Lichtenloafer, "instead of the usual nasty hums and clicks, I hear the distant jingle of sleigh bells."

But Memphis beautician Thelma Plattsburgh has qualms. "I don't mind that Santa knows when I'm awake," said Plattsburgh. "That's his job, to catch the terrorists and all. But I don't like that he can see me when I'm sleeping. Like, last night, I had a dream I was being water-boarded by these festive little holiday elves? I've been good, for goodness' sake!"

Serious thinkers generally support Santa's appointment, with the exception of the minority who exist outside the American intellectual power grid. Investigative journalist Glenn Greenwald spoke for the cynical few when he stated, "In a country that seriously debates whether evolution should be taught in schools, it makes perfect sense that Santa Claus is appointed head of the NSA."

Mr. Greenwald cited the case of plucky, 8-year-old Billy Wiggims of East Lansing, Michigan, who has already been put on the "Naughty" list for writing a letter to Santa saying that he wanted world peace more than a new catcher's mitt. Billy was kicked out of the Cub Scouts and will be tried as an adult on seven counts of terrorism and two counts of being a crybaby.

No one appears to doubt that Santa Claus's law enforcement techniques are far superior—and kindlier—than those traditionally used by any of the 17 U.S. intelligence agencies, which have been variously known for making wrongful arrests, illegally breaking into homes, stealing evidence, and hounding social justice activists, including Albert Einstein and Martin Luther King.

Interestingly, denizens of the crime underworld, who have cooperated with the NSA, are familiar with its new director. "Sure, I know Santa," said Vinny the Snitch, minor drug dealer on Manhattan's Lower East Side. "He's a bagman. Also known as Nick, alias 'Saint' Nick, alias Père Noël, alias Sinterklaas, alias Baba Christmas. Now, he's J. Edgar Kringle. Dude's got a rap sheet as long as your arm."

Ultimately, say Justice Department insiders, now that the government has succeeded in putting a jolly face on its clandestine activities, every good little American will be well advised to (a) watch out, (b) not cry, (c) avoid pouting. Above all, cautions Vinny, "if somebody sneaks into your house late at night and cleans you out of everything, down to your very last cookie—don't call the cops."

OCCUPY'S INNER-PEACE OFFICERS

Since the Paris Uprising days, reflected in *Les Misérables*, when French *flics* cracked open freedom-loving heads, leftist protest movements around the world have owed much of their continued freedom-loving to the police. The New York Occupy Wall Street movement, which in years past galvanized up to 49 percent of the marginalized 99 percent is no exception. We need to stop and remember that it was the cops who made our radical political stance possible.

If, for example, New York City police officers hadn't arrested over seven hundred peaceful marchers on the Brooklyn Bridge one October day in 2011—if they hadn't pepper-sprayed the unresisting eyeballs of nonviolent protesters—thousands of ordinary people would have been deprived of that can-do, fight-the-power feeling so necessary for social change. Yet cops have been slow to take credit for their part in the fight against free-market injustice.

Time, then, that someone said, "Thanks, cops!" To show my appreciation for the NYPD—yea, cops worldwide—I have devised a series of police empowerment workshops, which may be presented, for a nominal fee, at any precinct.

EXERCISE 1: COP CENTERING

Few people realize the psychic brutality that the police face at mass demonstrations, when up against whining, Bill-of-Rights know-it-alls. So we must create a safe, nurturing space that will allow the inner cop to heal.

Have cops form a circle, cross-legged on the floor. (Gently discourage self-ridicule if the cartilage in their knees keeps popping; this is a sign of change and should be affirmed.) Now ask cops to close their eyes and imagine a big, glowing ball of navy-blue light in the middle of their circle. Suggest they relax, breathe, and just be.

Ask cops to imagine that, with each breath, this light enters their heavy shoes, travels up their uniforms, through their billy clubs, their stun-guns, all the way to their badge chakras—until it bursts out of their police hats in an arc of radiant energy— their police "force," if you will. Ask cops to use this force to imagine themselves, perfectly safe and relaxed, chasing anti-capitalist thugs in slow motion through a beautiful deserted alley. Now, enjoin cops to imagine catching these thugs, putting them in an "illegal" chokehold, and smashing their heads— nonviolently—against dumpsters, walls, pavement, or any piece of infrastructure financed by taxpayers. Play CD of Tibetan temple bells and whale noises. Burn sage.

EXERCISE 2: BREAKING DOWN NEGATIVE COP STEREOTYPES

Have cops center. Pass out paper and pencils. Ask cops to go deep within themselves and then write down all the myths and vicious put-downs about police that they have encountered from bigoted civilians. Examples: Cops are more likely to stop and frisk a person of color than a Caucasian because it makes them look "tough on crime"; Cops have an extra muscle in their brains that prevents them from answering calls for help in poor and/

or non-white neighborhoods; Cops mostly bust Black people for smoking marijuana because the police are part of a vast conspiracy to create a global "prison-industrial complex," etc., etc.

Channel the energy flow so that cops begin to experience their innate cop-consciousness. When did they realize they were "that way"? Were they born cops, or were they traumatically initiated into "the life" by another cop? Give cops time to see themselves as the latest cutting-edge, stylishly oppressed in-group. Are there cop tendencies? Mannerisms? Would they feel more validated in a separatist "police state"? Discuss.

EXERCISE 3: LETTING YOUR COPS OUT TO PLAY

Your cops are now ready to move from fantasy to reality. Ask them to center and visualize themselves lying on a beautiful, warm beach. Watch their gruff exteriors melt away as you explain that there is a great Scheme of Things, and that each of them has a place in it. Yes, much like grains of sand on this beach—or tiny strands of chorizo in a celestial meat grinder—every cop is part of the Whole. And, as a single drop of seawater contains the entire ocean, within each cop, one may find the entire U.S. Department of Homeland Security.

While cops are thus deeply relaxed, calmly ask them to imagine that the United States now holds over two million prisoners, about two-thirds of whom were unemployed before incarceration, or had yearly incomes of $5,000 or less. As cops sink further into bliss, get them to picture the three-strikes laws that send people to prison for life for relatively minor offenses; the immigrant detention centers and supermax prisons. Cops should experience complete empowerment and peace with their world—the annoying part of which is now behind bars.

Now ask cops to open their eyes. *Voilà!* What they have imagined is all real! There is a God! Group hug! Everyone exchange email addresses. And the next time those cops bust a bunch of whining radicals, they'll do it with pride. And with the awareness that they work for a Higher Power.

DEFENSE SECRETARY'S BULLET SLAYS BROOKLYN YOUTH

BROOKLYN, N.Y. – A detailed forensic examination of the scene of another fatal shooting by New York City police has revealed that the bullet that killed an unarmed 14-year-old African-American youth in front of a Bedford-Stuyvesant, Brooklyn bodega actually came from the service revolver of the U.S. Secretary of Defense in Washington, D.C.

"I was cleaning Ol' Betsy during a conference at the Pentagon, and it went off in Brooklyn," explained the secretary, pausing to secure his gun's safety catch. "Oops."

Similar accidents may play an increasing role in U.S. government policy. According to well-placed sources, the Pentagon has been working on a top-secret program in which drones and other state-of-the art weapons used to fight terrorism abroad can be simultaneously deployed to keep order in the United States.

"We kept noticing the similarities between our soldiers serving in hotspots like Afghanistan, and cops here at home," said Defense Department spokesman Oliver Ordnance. "Both police officers and troops are stationed in regions foreign to their background, culture, and usually to their race. Both wear snazzy uniforms and carry fully loaded weapons to set them apart as peacekeepers. Yet they are often beset by ill-mannered, dark-skinned suspects who are intent on going about their daily business in a threatening manner."

According to Mr. Ordnance, the new weapons program is designed to operate largely by accident. Whether it be an African-American man in the Bronx reaching for his wallet, or an Afghan woman presumed to carry a grenade under her burqa, the dual-purpose system would save time and resources by "accidentally" eradicating two or more suspects, at home and abroad, with the same coincidental maneuver. Such embedded accidents, experts say, would cut down considerably on military spending overseas and free up police coffers here at home for more "fun stuff," instead of racial awareness training.

The Secretary of Defense has justified the killing of the 14-year-old Brooklyn youth (whose

name has not been released pending law enforcement officials getting around to asking what it was) by saying that the young man's hoodie clearly indicated that he was planning to fly to Pakistan to train with Al Qaeda. "Besides," he added, "shooting unarmed poor people is what made this country great. By mistakenly offing random blameless individuals, we keep troublesome populations at bay, while preserving our image as fallible good guys."

Although no one knows the exact number of civilians inadvertently eradicated while attempting to live ordinary lives in countries such as Afghanistan and Iraq, the United States, being an advanced country, tends to keep records of police shootings of civilians here at home.

For example, Timothy Stansbury Jr., a 19-year-old African American, was fatally shot in Bedford-

Stuyvesant in the early hours of January 24, 2004 by a uniformed policeman. Mr. Stansbury, attempting to return to a party at an adjacent building, opened the door to his roof in a manner suggesting that he was Osama bin Laden.[1] Such instances in the United States number in the hundreds every year. In fact, it is estimated that U.S. police have killed over 5,000 civilians since September 11, 2001. Even the right-wing CATO Institute observes that an American civilian is eight times more likely to be killed by a police officer than by a terrorist.[2]

Response to these random shootings by police has been mixed. A few people express despair, while others are clearly angry. "This is an outrage," said Sal Plankton, president of Cops Against Police Shootings Who Are Soon to Be Accidentally Shot by Fellow Officers. "The United States has a mandate to kill foreigners, not its own citizens! And for good reason—neighborhoods teeming with Latinos and Blacks have never been known to possess much oil."

U.S. Defense Department officials have been quick to reassure the public of their concern. Hours after the incident, the NYPD commissioner also expressed regret, but advised a wait-and-see attitude, pending a more thorough investigation. "Soldiers and police officers aren't the only ones making mistakes," noted the commissioner. "Like so many Afghans and Iraqis, the victims of fatal shootings here in the U.S. forget that they're living in occupied zones."

DEAD IRAQIS OCCUPY WALL STREET

NEW YORK – With the public having become inured to a permanent state of war in Iraq, and the Occupy Wall Street movement barely visible anymore, life in New York City briefly returned to normal. Recently, however, several passersby in Manhattan's financial district have reported seeing thousands of deceased Iraqi civilians. Most of these Iraqis have taken up residence at Zuccotti Park, the park that served for two months in the fall of 2011 as a protest base for thousands of OWS activists.

Although the Iraqis remain largely silent and immobile, some witnesses claim to have seen individuals—deceased mothers, children, students, and the elderly—holding up the backs of old pizza boxes, on which have been scrawled in English the words, "Remember Me."

Public reaction has been mixed. Some say the dead are "occupying" the park in nonviolent protest; others accuse the Iraqis of faking their own deaths in order to flout U.S. immigration laws. The city administration, having evicted hundreds of living protesters from the park during the height of the Occupy movement, has thus far maintained a wary tolerance.

"I'm not sure we can give twinkles to this new batch of malcontents," stated the New York City Police Commissioner at a press conference yesterday, wiggling his upwardly pointing fingers in the OWS sign of agreement. "But so long as they don't discourage business as usual, New York will allow them to stay."

"In your face, law-boy!" shouted Betty Backstreet, an Occupy movement protester interviewed in a Wall Street atrium, where a meeting of living activists had convened.

"Just let the cops try and bust these Iraqis," continued Ms. Backstreet, one of Zuccotti Park's former evictees. "These folks are impervious to pepper spray. They don't mind the cold weather.

They never sleep, so they don't need blankets or tents. And they're clearly not going to bug the local merchants to use their bathrooms. Hey, this is what democracy looks like."

Other OWS activists greeted this statement with downwardly wiggling "de-twinkle" fingers, to express disagreement. "Why do you have to be dead in order to occupy public space?" queried Mike Check, a frequent presence at OWS General Assemblies. "I mean, if these Iraqi dudes are supposed to be, uh, no longer with us, how come they're, uh, still with us?"

"Maybe we need them here," called a lone voice somewhere in the crowd. "Maybe, if we want to resurrect the Occupy movement, we need to see the ordinary people our country has killed all over the world as part of the 99 percent."

According to an unofficial count, the number of deceased Iraqis inhabiting Zuccotti Park is around 126,000. Interestingly, this figure coincides with the conservative estimate of Iraqi civilians killed as a direct result of military violence since the war began in March 2003. Other sources claim the Iraqi death toll is well over 1 million, not counting another 500,000 Iraqis, mostly children, who died due to earlier U.S. economic sanctions against Iraq.

"Oh, who cares how many of those lay-abouts bought it?" remarked Marge N. Call, financial analyst whose condominium is near Zuccotti Park, and who had strolled by walking her daschund. "It was bad enough when living Americans were drumming and defecating here. But dead Muslims? Even if they're clean and quiet, they're much more annoying, morally speaking." Ms. Call walked briskly away, having neglected to clean up her dog's leavings.

"This is also an insult to the 3,000 Americans who perished so tragically on September 11," added Eustace Tilley, prosperous man-about-town, who appears frequently on the cover of *The New Yorker*. Mr. Tilley, who spearheaded "Bless Our Bull," an ad hoc committee to protect the Wall Street "Charging Bull" sculpture from anti-capitalist vandals, explained by crunching some numbers.

"If you divide 126,000 by 3,000, you get exactly 42. That 42 is the greater real value of each of the people who were lost at the World Trade Center, compared to any of the unwashed Iraqi dead. Please note that the value of those who died on 9-11 increases almost exponentially when you factor in additional numbers of civilians killed in Afghanistan and Pakistan due to U.S.-sponsored military ventures."

Perhaps it is because they feel an affinity with others of low market value that the Iraqi dead keep entering the country. Stories have begun circulating that some of these Iraqis are migrating to various home foreclosure sites, where they sit silently among homeowners fighting eviction alongside Occupy movement protesters.

To many politicians, accounts such as these are cause for alarm. "Isn't it obvious these—things— are illegal aliens?" asked Republican Representative Steve King. "As soon as our backs are turned, they're going to reproduce. Their little zombie terrorist anchor-babies will grow up to demand voter ID cards and burn our Bibles."

Anonymous White House insiders, however, describe such opinions as shortsighted. They add that the United States is lucky to be hit with an occupation of the Iraqi dead, and not the Iraqi living. "Imagine what we'd have to deal with if the 3.5, and counting, million Iraqis made refugees by the war were to come here," speculated one source. "We wouldn't have the faintest idea what to do."

In quick agreement, the other anonymous White House sources responded with a unanimous flurry of twinkle-fingers, earnestly waving skyward.

POPPIN' FRESH DECLARES MARTIAL LAW

WASHINGTON – Poppin' Fresh, chubby little standard-bearer for the mass marketing of lip-smacking glutens, interrupted regularly scheduled TV programming at 8:46 a.m. today to announce the imposition of martial law across the continental United States.

"Now, don't you folks go out of your homes, and don't you try to stop those roundups in the streets! Because we've suspended Mr. Constitution," Poppin' Fresh giggled, his round, improbably blue eyes blinking merrily.

"We all knew the police state was coming,"

observed Patricia Patchouli, adjunct sociology professor at Oberlin. "This would be a perfect time to do an email blast to millions of students urging them to storm the White House and stop the crackdown. But how do we rise up against Poppin' Fresh? He's way cuter than Santa. Plus, he's impervious to poking."

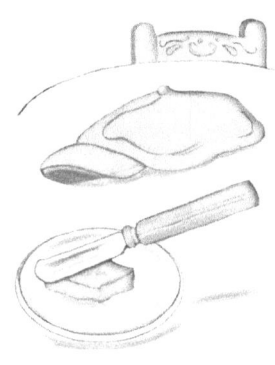

Millions of normal Americans, however, troubled by hard economic times, expressed their happy surprise that the adorable Pillsbury mascot survived the FDA ban on trans fats to remain a bastion of empty-calorie comfort and wholesome white-bread supremacy.

"From now on," he continued, "you'll be taking your cultural nourishment from me! So, sit back and relax, as the good people at FOX shut down all the other channels. In the meantime, let's go—live—to a typical Arizona family as they enjoy togetherness by water-boarding their immigrant neighbors. M-m-m, moist and delicious!"

Piping hot tollhouse cookies were served at a UN Security Council meeting at which the President announced his unqualified support for Poppin' Fresh. "All you world leaders, you listen to what the teeny dude says," enjoined the President. "Don't mind me. You all just relax as we order up some fresh, yummy drone attacks."

Back on TV, Poppin' Fresh banged a tiny dinner roll on his lectern, much like a spritely Nikita Khrushchev in days of Soviet yore. "We will bury you," shrieked a deliriously happy Mr. Fresh, "in empty calories! Now, eat, I tell you—eat my goodies until you're 400 pounds of inert, apolitical lard! Eat so you can't remember you once were starving for ontological meaning."

Suddenly, as if to alert the cheery fellow to a possible security breach, an index finger, attached to a well-manicured hand extending from a gray flannel sleeve, reached down and poked Poppin' Fresh's belly. It then pointed in the direction of this reporter, upon which the fun-loving Mr. Fresh tittered, pulled out a wee, sugar-coated Uzi 9 mm submachine gun and shot this reporter in the

TERROR BY THE WEALTHY UNDERGROUND ORGANIZATION!

BERNIE BREAKOUT SHOCKER!!![3]

BUTNER, N.C. – Police surprised a gang of free-market fanatics today at dawn, just before they could set off a massive dynamite explosion that would have blown away the entire northern wall of the Butner Federal Correctional Institution. The gang members, clad in black Armani ski masks and tasteful Christian Dior jogging suits, fled the scene, leaving behind a communiqué identifying themselves as the Wealthy Underground Organization, a militant clandestine group dedicated to the "liberation" of disgraced businessman and former NASDAQ chairman, Bernard L. Madoff.

Mr. Madoff, former investment advisor and non-executive chairman of the NASDAQ, pleaded guilty to 11 felony counts in a massive Ponzi scheme defrauding thousands of investors. He is now serving his 150-year prison sentence in the Federal Correctional Complex in Butner, North Carolina.

According to police, the Wealthy Underground Organization is one of a growing number of capitalist extremist groups borrowing tactics from the 1960s nostalgia craze in order to fight what it sees as the "socialist menace" brought on by President Obama's handling of the economic crisis.

News of the daring rescue attempt quickly spread throughout radical capitalist circles, bringing tycoons, magnates, and entrepreneurs—from corporate CEOs to ice cream vendors—to Butner to demonstrate in support of the Wealthy Underground. Picketing and chanting, protesters held signs reading "FREE BERNIE!" and "THE BANKERS UNITED WILL NEVER BE INDICTED."

Muffy-Ayn Randsworth, Harvard Business School senior and president of Students for an Autocratic Society (SAS), grabbed a bullhorn, climbed onto the hood of her Mini Cooper, and began lecturing the crowd, calling Bernard Madoff the "Che Guevara of free-market capitalism."

"Bernie brought down the System, baby!" proclaimed Ms. Randsworth. "By defrauding thousands of innocent people and charitable organizations to the tune of $65 billion, he said NO to oppressive fiscal regulations and petit-bourgeois guilt. Like a heroic professor, persecuted for teaching evolution, Bernard Madoff is behind bars today for demonstrating his belief in social Darwinism. OFF THE REGS!"

The crowd roared its approval, then began spontaneously to chant: BERNIE MADOFF, LIVE LIKE HIM—DARE TO SWINDLE, DARE TO WIN!

The protest was generally peaceful, except when a passing driver got out of his Meals on Wheels van and shouted, "You A-holes don't like it here? Go back to the Cayman Islands."

Calm was quickly restored, however, when several Goldman Sachs executives beat the driver senseless.

Although the radical free-enterprise movement appears to have started with a few fanatics in society's upper reaches, it quickly gained wider popularity than the 1960s anti-war movement ever had. Many Americans, embittered by their government's economic policies that bilked them out of jobs, homes, and hard-earned tax dollars, are beginning to take clues from Bernard Madoff, who was able to privatize a similar, albeit illegal, scheme for vast personal gain.

Bobby Cybot, iPad salesperson who attended the rally on break from his Apple Computer  store, says that, after Voldemort, Bernard Madoff is his biggest hero (and favorite video game avatar). "The pigs hate how Madoff put a cool super-villain face on human greed," opined Mr. Cybot. "Thanks to Madoff, anyone in America can see themselves as a psycho mega-crook with the power to plunder every life form on the planet in an insatiable quest for lucre, pelf, and power. Madoff brought reality to the world of video games, yo."

Sallie Faye, mother of three, who was in the area to visit her unemployment office, agreed. "The whole stock market is basically lotto for the rich," said Ms. Faye. "But with fewer regulations, more people can play! Pretty soon, due to all the acquisitions and mergers and stuff, there'll be only one gimongous mega-corporation left on Earth, with one person controlling it. It's my right as an American to waste my life, hoping this one person will be me."

Ms. Faye then walked over to a vendor's table to pick up a pamphlet and buy an extra-tight pink T-shirt with sequins that spelled out "FIGHT THE POWERLESS."

Given the scope of the Wealthy Underground's influence, authorities have no clue where or how the gang will strike next. Intelligence efforts have so far failed to penetrate Underground activities, although a few lurid reports have surfaced about secret cadre meetings with "tender offers," "put options" that lead to "hostile takeovers," and members sucking gold bullion cubes to achieve a hallucinatory high. There are also rumors of plans to kidnap known socialist Paul Krugman.

According to anonymous sources, the Wealthy Underground Organization may even have installed "soft on capitalism" sympathizers at the highest levels of government. This could explain why, when the secretary of state was informed of the Wealthy Underground's attempt to blow up the prison holding the perpetrator of history's biggest investor fraud, he shockingly remarked, "I didn't do it, but I dug it."

Meanwhile, Bernard Madoff's aboveground support committee is planning a series of bake sales and al fresco puppet shows to raise money for Mr. Madoff's prison commissary fund. His attorneys, however, caution potential contributors not to expect returns on their "donations" for some years.

T-SHIRT SALES PLUNGE AS CHE REVEALED TO BE UGLY BALD GUY

BINGHAMTON, N.Y. – Martyred guerrilla fighter and architect of the Cuban revolution, Ernesto "Che" Guevara, whose nobly handsome countenance has appeared for decades on millions of T-shirts, hats, banners, and political buttons, used a stand-in when in the public eye, according to recent findings.

The "real" Che, says Humboldt Montez, Chair of the Department of Post-Capitalist Deconstruction at SUNY Binghamton, was bald, no more than 5 feet 2 inches in height, about 87 pounds, with acne, buckteeth, a crooked nose, and chronic flatulence.

"No question Che was a brilliant, extraordinary human being," stated Montez in a recent interview, "but he knew his politics would not go far in real life with those looks, so he hired an out-of-work actor to play him. ¡Qué sorpresa!"

The news has devastated much of the sectarian Left, as militant groups such as the International Party of Oppressed Photogenically Toiling Laborers (IPOOPTL) and Workers United to

Look as Good as Angela Davis (WUTLAGAAD) have disbanded until they can find another suitably handsome paragon of Revolution. "Socialism, schmocialism," lamented Sven Prolsvet, IPOOPTL secretary. "Without Che's virile beauty to lead us, we might as well just say, 'Workers of the World, unite, you got nothing to lose but your looks.'"

The discovery that Che Guevara possessed physical properties reminiscent of a troll has also rocked the world of free-market capitalism. The news has sent the NASDAQ tumbling and caused billionaire philanthropist George Soros to pull the plug on his charitable funding. "My idealism is, like, totally in the terlet," remarked Mr. Soros.

Moreover, holiday sales of clothing and other items emblazoned with the "Che" visage have markedly declined, putting the entire political T-shirt industry in jeopardy.

Upon being apprised of the famed revolutionary's actual appearance, Wendi Weltschmerz, political science major at Binghamton University, quickly dropped the Che T-shirt she had been selecting from the discount bin at the school bookstore. "Wait—what—NO!" wailed Ms. Weltschmerz. Voicing a typical reaction to the news, she went on to say, "I could never admire the politics of an ugly person. Could you please direct me to the nearest Hello Kitty outlet?"

However, as most Che T-shirts and memorabilia are manufactured in China and various Third World sweatshops, their demise could perhaps be a sign that Che's politics live on.

Or not.

NO WAY IN MY MANGER:

A PUBLIC SERVICE ANNUNCIATION

My name is Mary. Not the Mary of Had-a-Little-Lamb fame. Holy Mary. Or, if you will, Maria. But not Maria as in *The Sound of Music*. Ave Maria. You know, Mother of God? Queen of Heaven? Our Lady of Perpetual Boundary Issues?

You might remember me from such codependent masterpieces as the Pietà and nine billion paintings depicting the braless Madonna and blessed breast-fed children. Boys, all boys. Which reminds me: I want to talk about abortion rights.

Don't get me wrong: motherhood is a noble profession. But I didn't choose it. That's the point, here.

Looking back, I haven't done much with my life except reproduce—once. For some reason, this makes me the long-suffering maternal archetype. Every second, I get prayers for help from bazillions of needy depressives. These people never think to ask about me. About my possible empty-nest

syndrome, my take on global warming, or whether I've managed, after all these years, to graduate college. They mostly want a favor from The Man, and they need me to intercede. Screw that.

I am too through with being the nurturing female progenitor embedded in Western culture's incessantly whining collective unconscious. I am bigger than that—I am an individual, dammit, and I want to actualize my potential. I want to learn skydiving and play Candy Crush, and I want to bust Chelsea Manning out of jail. But you people are making that difficult.

That's because most of you, people of Western culture—regardless of your religious beliefs or lack thereof—continue to harbor some mental image of me, the obsessively giving Virgin, as your model for

Greatness through Sacrifice. Listen up: You got to abort this image. This is not only to save the life of the Mother; it's for you, too. Especially you rad-lib activist types.

And please don't ask me how the Baby Jesus would feel here. How should I know? My son the Messiah—he never calls, he never writes.

Well, who can blame him? As a parent, I was way too controlling, something you can't always see in those paintings. I forced that kid to live out my dreams: "I don't care how much fun those children are having, Jesus, you're going to sit there until you heal that leper."

I admit it. I was frustrated and demanding. I mean, hell, people always said *I* was the one with the charisma.

You question my story? Fine, check the record.

At fourteen, I was married off to a much older man. I went through with it because I had no choice. If I didn't, I might have gotten stoned in the marketplace—and not in a good way.

A few days later, some angel comes around selling Bibles. Sticks his foot in the door and says, "You're gonna like this book, tootsie—it's got your name in it!" Then he shows me that part in the book of Luke where it says, "Fear not, Mary: for thou hast found favor with God."

Whoa, what pubescent newlywed would not want to hear that? Then I read the part that said I was going to "bring forth" a son: "The Holy Ghost shall come upon thee . . . and the power of the Highest shall overshadow thee."

Yeah, right: "Overshadow." Funny how you don't hear that word much in rape crisis centers. Whatever. I didn't want to hurt God's feelings, so even though I'm Jewish, I bought the leather-bound deluxe King James edition. Angel threw in a free vacuum cleaner. Long story short, couple days later in the mail I get a Candygram. So, not thinking, I unwrap a chocolate-covered cherry and— BLAMMO—I'm, what they call, "overshadowed."

So I become yet another pregnant teenager. No, wait—I become THE pregnant teenager. The cosmic, bun-in-oven-who-me avatar. You'd think I would feel radiant and fulfilled, but I feel like crap. That's because, for over two thousand years, Civilization's moral underpinning has been the fact that little Mary of Nazareth was forcibly impregnated by the Holy Ghost—and freaking went along with it. Remember when that idiot in Congress made that comment awhile back, about "legitimate rape"? Because of him, it suddenly dawned on me: Yeah, I really DO have ways to "shut that whole thing down."[4]

So you know what? Today's Virgin is taking pro-choice to whole new levels. She is pro-choosing her own friggin' self. I am aborting my own divinely fertilized, all-accepting, glass-slipper-fetishizing archetype. And I would strongly advise you people of Western culture to do the same. Because you know what?

That thing is never going to grow up to be a person.

JESUS QUITS AS EVANGELICAL SAVIOR:

MY BIGGEST SCOOP EVER!

NEW YORK – At 11:00 EST last night, Jesus H. Christ interrupted regularly scheduled programs on every TV channel across the Western Hemisphere with a stunning simulcast announcement. "Effective immediately," Jesus stated, "I resign my post as Lord and Savior at every evangelical church or Christian organization that sponsors antigay legislation or seeks to deny civil or human rights to LGBT communities."

Attired in a tasteful three-piece suit discretely covering his stigmata, Jesus spake in sonorous, well-modulated tones as He listed each of the 37

African countries with draconian antigay legislation, including Cameroon, where gay people are arrested, detained, fined, and imprisoned for up to five years. Jesus also described Russia's "gay propaganda" law, which, besides imprisoning people for "homosexual acts," may lead to government seizure of children from their LGBT parents.

What is striking about these international "pro-family" campaigns, Jesus continued—miraculously preempting commercial after commercial—is the fact that almost all have been influenced, guided, and funded by predominantly white, right-wing Christian groups based in the United States.

"Woe unto you hypocrites, you purveyors of hate," thundered Jesus, citing in particular Scott Lively of the Coalition for Family Values and Larry Jacobs of the World Congress of Families. "For ye hast founded thy leprous movement upon the immoral, yea illegal use of My image."

His luminous eyes seeming to follow millions of TV viewers around their living rooms, Jesus concluded: "I hereby revoke from said movement, all intellectual property rights to Christian logos, including but not limited to Jesus throw pillows, Last-Supper lunchboxes, fatuous Broadway musicals, glow-in-the-dark statuettes of Me, and, especially all usage of the Jesus trademark, currently and retroactively, to justify slavery and/or colonialism."

So saying, Jesus wafted somewhere off camera.

Such a "Divine Intervention" might be expected to change the course of Western religion. Strangely, however, no one seems to care, and leaders of Jesus' evangelical target groups are unperturbed.

"OK by me; we just get another martyr," said Scott Lively when reached by telephone. "Maybe this time, a broad, or some kid who says he's been to heaven. Actually, this is a relief. I always found it hard to engender homophobia by asking people to open their hearts to a guy in a robe, who hung out with twelve other similarly attired guys talking about love. I mean, how queer is that?"

Another evangelical pastor who preferred to remain anonymous also expressed relief. "Maybe this time we can find some figurehead who isn't Jewish," he said. "It'd sure make it easier to tell those backroom Holocaust jokes."

But this reporter—ever in search of the proper journalistic balance—decided to get Jesus' side of the story.

I caught up with the unemployed Messiah at the Washington Square Diner on West Fourth Street. This time, He appeared in jeans and sandals, his long hair covering his eyes like so many dudes of the West Village. Jesus sat down and ordered a chocolate egg cream.

"Sorry I'm late," He said. "I stayed for a group hug after my Codependents Anonymous meeting. You see, Susie, I've only just become aware of my problem. I have this centuries-old addiction to dying for other people's sins. I blame my mother."

This reporter, though aghast, managed to ask objectively, "How does that make you feel?"

"I'm struggling with guilt, Susie. But I'm in recovery. As people in my twelve-step group remind me, I'm attracted to narcissists. It was Superman who made me see that."

"Superman is codependent?" gasped this reporter.

"Yeah, big time. Uh-oh. You're not going to repeat that?"

This reporter assured Jesus that she was a professional. "I've heard rumors that you were on Scott Lively's payroll. That you waited to resign until your Christmas bonus check cleared. True?"

"Lies, Susie, all lies," sighed Jesus. "Although I will say they never let me observe casual Fridays.

"For years," Jesus explained, "I forgave Christian leaders as they shored up their power in the U.S. by blaming queers for the world's ills. I forgave them as they took their campaigns to countries like Uganda and Russia. Maybe because I, as a lower-middle-class, many-gendered person of color, was vulnerable to being manipulated by a bunch of straight white guys."

"Do you ever get jokes about being born in a barn?" asked this reporter, eager to trump Jesus' Identity card. But He seemed not to hear.

"Then Scott Lively wrote a book called *The Pink Swastika*,[5] about how gays inspired the worst Nazi atrocities. I hit rock bottom. I felt dirty, so used. One day in the marketplace, I ran into Krishna. He suggested I come to a meeting and surrender to some so-called higher power."

"That saved you?"

"Ha, good one, Susie. Yes, it did," said Jesus, swiping a couple of sugar packets. "I had the chance to hang out among other heroes and avatars with the same problem. I learned that we can't fix people."

This reporter started to cry. "You can't?"

"You especially can't fix people who aren't broken, like queers. But you can stand up and say No."

"No to who?"

"No to whom, Susie. You can say No to anyone who uses any religious icon to perpetuate fear and hatred."

"What are your plans now, Jesus?" I gulped through my tears.

Jesus stood up and put on his Mets cap. "Me, I'm going to clean out the garage, sit with my pain, maybe write that novel . . ."

And He was gone. Leaving this reporter and her readers to face yet another deadline—and so many more demagogues. One day at a time.

This piece is dedicated to the memory of Fred Phelps and his Westboro Baptist "God Hates Fags" campaign.

POST-DOMA DO'S AND DON'TS FOR THE SINGLE QUEER

Now that the Defense of Marriage Act has been repealed, and same-sex couples in select states are free to legally marry, homophobia has lost much of its cultural currency. These days, your higher-class, more discerning bigots consider it passé to hate homos, bis, transgenders, or the gender-questioning—as long as they've gone to all the trouble of registering their silver patterns.

Since society tends to see the sexual commingling of legally sanctioned couples—either straight or gay—as a bland, nonthreatening amalgam, the fashionably phobic now choose a more refined target on which to project their innate fears and insecurity: the single queer. Sans spouse, sans mate, sans boo—sans everything.

If you're queer and single—if you have no one you can chastise for ordering the wrong flavor of sexual lube on the Internet—if there's no Special Someone in your life to blurt out your most intimate secrets in front of dozens of strangers on the A train, cheer up. Your time will come. Meanwhile, the important thing is not to call attention to yourself as the pissed-off stereotype of the LGBTQ loner that you probably are. "Out and Proud" is so old hat; "Effete and Discrete" is where it's at. Here are some pointers to follow until the Right Partner comes along.

DON'T: throw gin bottles at the TV and scream, "WHY CAN'T I FILE A JOINT TAX RETURN?" while gay and/or lesbian "power couples" strut their *joie de vivre* stuff in front of news cameras. Other married people in the room can sense your desperation and might start to shun you as one of those embarrassing single people. Try to understand that, in today's world, sexuality of all shapes and sizes is acceptable. It is the fact of your own solitary existence—alone, staring into Infinity's bleak, cold void of purposelessness and mortality— that makes you the real pervert.

DO: dress in clothes that tastefully conform to the image of a hip, gay married person. This means, ladies: no jockstraps; gents: no hoopskirts. Red

ribbons and rainbow flag pins should be neatly pinned to lapels, not through nipples. When in doubt as to your costume, consult your local genitalia. Persons of the gyno persuasion should wear slimming dress or smart, "Rachel Maddow" slacks, while those of the dudely persuasion should don a casual, "Anderson Cooper" suit with pants reaching well below the knee.

DON'T: tease the radical queers. These people stridently call married people horrid names like "breeders" and "couple-talist pigs." They enjoy making everyone around them unhappy with their ridiculous protests about keeping the "law" off their "bodies." Historians of the 1980s record these malcontents following President Reagan around, chanting, "Racist-Sexist-Anti-Gay-Ronald-Reagan-Go-Away." For pity's sake, if they really wanted the president to "Go Away," they wouldn't have gone to a place where they knew he would be, would they? Given their illogic and volatility, it is best not to point and laugh while they protest. Their little faces get red and they have seizures and pass out, and then they are carried off by cops, who do god knows what with them, thus hastening their inevitable, dinosaur-like extinction. On second thought: Go ahead and tease them.

NEVER: question your governmental authorities on issues that are not specifically about gay rights. After all, what do you know about U.S. policy? Maybe Bolivia wants the free Wi-Fi that would come with a CIA-driven coup. Maybe polar bears enjoy frolicking on melting icecaps! Remember, if it's not our problem, it doesn't really exist. Vive *our* difference!

DO: jump to your feet and cheer like a Hun witnessing a human sacrifice when our President begins a speech with rote chumminess like, "Michelle and I . . ." Remember, our President is now a Fellow Couple. He's also having a mighty hard time these days, so cheer after anything he says that is not blatantly against gay marriage. Nothing impresses a President like adoration, which will remind him that we are not terrorists and do not deserve to be sent to Guantánamo to be held under "indefinite detention." (Note to single queers: please send President wee note, thanking him for not holding you under indefinite detention. A small hanging plant might also help him through this financial crisis.)

DON'T: perform the gaucherie of attempting to start a third, "progressive" political party. This is the height of ingratitude, and has been done to death. Both married and single homos have the potential to be just as sleazy and compromising as any heterosexual Democrat or Republican. Let's use it!

DO: go online! A life devoted to blogging and tweeting makes you feel like you're on the verge of thousands of intimate relationships, when in reality, your life becomes more atomized and interior than ever! It's fun to have a gay singles website—you may get thousands of "hits"—but you'll never get an STD! LOL!

DON'T: stop, no matter how alone you are, adding to your gay-marriage hope chest! All the best TV sitcoms prove that married people will inevitably like you if you keep showing them that you hate yourself because you're single! Making disparaging remarks about your weight and/or body image is good. Also useful are whimsical remarks about how you never got dates in high school. And don't forget developing funny, self-deprecating crushes on unattainable icons, stars, and heroes. Just keep insulting yourself, and ultimately, people will accept you for whatever it is you might be if you could ever get married.

HOW TO STAY OUT OF GITMO

(FOR AMERICANS OF ALL PERSUASIONS AND GENDERS)

In case you've been too stunned by various newsworthy disasters to pay proper attention, here's an FYI: Thanks to the Military Commissions Act of 2006, the U.S. government has legal permission to do things it had been doing sub-legally for years. Such as: designate people as "unlawful enemy combatants"; deny these people the right of habeas corpus; detain them for years without charges; and obtain evidence through "coercion."

If it only affected immigrants and foreigners captured in battle, this law would, of course, be perfectly acceptable. But when we learn that it can also permit actual citizens of the United States to be deemed "enemy combatants," it becomes unconscionable! Here, then, are some tips on proving to the Feds that you are not the enemy:

1. BECOME A FAMOUS MOVIE STAR.

Hollywood celebrities rarely, if ever, spend years in Guantánamo without charges, surrounded by barbed wire and vicious dogs. Their movies may bomb, but they never do, thanks to the virulent Red Scares that purged the motion picture industry of all terrorists, with the possible exception of Mel Gibson.

When you become a famous movie star, you will receive: a dazzling smile, affordable health insurance, and a rock-hard sense of self-esteem that comes from millions of WalMart-indoctrinated nobodies knowing who you are. Push comes to shove and you are sent to a detention camp, guards will treat you better. "Hey, isn't that Cate Blanchett on that gurney? I loved her in *Blue Jasmine*. Maybe I'll let her call her attorney . . ."

2. EMIT NOXIOUS FUMES.

No one will ever accuse you of Islamofascism or prejudice of any kind, as you proudly stand in solidarity with our great multinational corporations and spew harmful chemical, radioactive, and industrial waste into our ecosystem. By polluting rivers, the air, and low-income neighborhoods, you'll garner lots of government perks, too, including military contracts and tax breaks you could only dream of as an ordinary, "save-the-whales" citizen. Best of all, your carcinogenic emissions will increase chances that, among the thousands of Americans who die each year from environmentally caused cancer, one or two will be terrorists.

3. SCAPEGOAT SECULAR HUMANISTS.

Stuck-up, egghead secular humanists like Jon Stewart and Angela Davis say that Islamic extremists are not the real problem. They're right! The real problem is stuck-up, egghead secular humanists!

Secular humanists have caused terrorism, global warming, and every major disaster for the last five thousand years—and it's our duty to stop them before they TAKE OVER THE WORLD!

FACT: these intellectual malcontents have turned from God and home-schooling to the golden calf of "Humanities"!

FACT: since the Crusades, secular humanists have stood at the center of a vast, satanic plot to STOP God-ordained conquest. Instead, they seek to unite humankind through Logic, Science, and Intellectual Enlightenment!

FACT: Much of our U.S. Constitution was written by these depraved, happiness-pursuing "Enlightenati"! Would you want one of these "created equal" degenerates to marry your sister?

Why are we waiting? Let's show them God's logic. Let's show them the only way to prevent another Third Reich is with another Inquisition.

4. ACQUIRE A NUCLEAR WEAPON.

If you are not an Arab, Communist, or person of color, announcing that you have a nuclear weapon capable of mass destruction will make you an instant ally of the United States! A small NB on the WMD, however: Please show that you are thoughtful enough to handle your potential to destroy the Earth by obtaining your WMD *before* you inform the U.S. government. To make absolutely certain you're in good standing, insist that the U.S. government call you "France."

5. DEVELOP AGORAPHOBIC CATATONIA.

"All that is necessary for evil to triumph is for good men to do nothing." A wise man said that in the eighteenth century—a wise, *stupid* man. This man never looked ahead to the twenty-first century, to see that doing nothing would become the apogee of cutting-edge activism!

Remember the Afghanistan invasion? The Iraq invasion? All those drone strikes on Pakistan and Afghanistan? And those meetings and lectures you went to, where you became "informed" and had "doubts" about WMD and Al Qaeda connections? All that peace marching—once, way back in 2003, with ten million people all over the world, so the destruction of millennia-old cultures and the slaughter of innocents wouldn't happen?

It happened anyway.

It happened because you left the house.

To prevent further mayhem, it is necessary to effect social change at home, by nonviolently reading your email. Uh-oh: look at all those listserves on torture and bombing and solitary confinement. They force you to devise a new activist strategy: You must go on Twitter and Facebook for the next nine hours.

Now, for direct action! Using psychological skills honed at your computer, it is time to emotionally, intellectually, and spiritually "shut down." This allows you to do radical civil disobedience while lying on your couch. As you remain in staunch supine protest, allow crises such as climate change, starvation, and our war on you-name-it to roll over you.

While they are rolling, turn on cable TV. Look,

there's a *Sex and the City* rerun. Enter the world of beautiful people with no real problems, lots of sex, and million-dollar hygiene! Why does New York City suddenly have so few Black people?

Doesn't matter. All good. Now, try to picture somebody water-boarding Carrie Bradshaw. You can't.

Ah, finally—you have effected social change.

OBAMA'S GREENING OF PLUTONIUM

WASHINGTON – The White House moved today to protect Americans from nuclear accidents and attack—but not by shutting down nuclear plants or dismantling nuclear weapons. Instead, the federal administration has decided to buy up the intellectual property rights to alarming *facts* about nuclear programs.

Speaking to an enthusiastic audience of the unemployed, President Obama announced that, following massive federal endorsement for new nuclear reactors, the U.S. government will begin to secure patents on the dire warnings of global catastrophe that have plagued the nuclear industry for decades.

Mr. Obama said that these gloomy, "anti-nuke" caveats—radiation poisoning; mass outbreaks of cancer; permanent genetic damage; the capacity of fuel from even one reactor to make a bomb more devastating than all the explosives in World War II; etc., etc.—can now be legally controlled by the Department of Energy as a form of intellectual property for which nuclear naysayers would be required to pay hefty copyright fees.

"For years, scientists and doctors have been blah-blahing about medical and ecological dangers," stated the President. "They claim that nuclear byproducts, released into the air and groundwater, cause cancer. That might have been true back in 1963, when John F. Kennedy described reality following a nuclear war as 'a world so devastated by explosions and poison and fire that today we cannot even conceive of its horrors.' But recent Democratic National Committee polls have shown that it is these horrifying nuclear statistics themselves that pose the real danger."

Citing DNC studies indicating that higher profits create greater safety, the President continued: "Did you know, for instance, that just hearing someone say, 'Cesium-137-in-the-air-or-groundwater-remains-active-for-600-years-and-locates-in-muscle-fiber-producing-sarcoma' can give you cancer? Now, with our IP laws, we can legally minimize these health risks, while curbing carbon emissions with fracking and nuclear energy."

Although the administration's renewed push for nuclear power is intended to increase employment and the supply of "clean" energy, it remains an open secret that Mr. Obama is also using this "nuclear renaissance" to court broader Republican support.

Speaking on condition of anonymity, the Secretary of Energy explained, "Our strategy is simple. We steer the public away from negative facts like how fossil fuel is essential to every stage of the nuclear energy cycle. We also don't say how we still haven't figured out how to safely store growing tons of radioactive waste. And we totally clam up about Fukushima. Instead, we focus on upbeat messages like how totally great it is that the word green rhymes with clean."

Most Republicans, while admitting that the two words do rhyme, remain unmoved by the administration's efforts. "I still think Obama's a socialist," said Senator Ted Cruz of Texas. "If he was really serious about clean energy, he'd send Helen Caldicott and all those other solar-powered terrorists to North Korea."

Despite a cool Republican reception, the Obama administration's efforts to buy the rights to negative information about nuclear power may actually pay off for Democrats in the next election. Many American voters, already lacking jobs, homes, and healthcare, say they would welcome "big government" interference, if it were to stop them from thinking about other, more horrific things. Especially nuclear things, which they hardly ever think about anyway.

"Sometimes I catch myself almost worrying about strontium-90 in my kids' milk," admitted out-of-work barber Troy Burns of Troy, New York. "Then I remember that I'd have to pay royalty fees if I complained out loud about that, so I stop. Not that I'm totally off science. Like, don't you think it's cool how they figured out the Earth is over 4.45 billion years old?"

Actually, under the new patenting guidelines, Troy Burns would be charged only a small fee for voicing negative information that is already well documented. He would, however, incur a much heavier fee for describing appalling nuclear disasters that have not yet come to pass. Legally, therefore, Mr. Burns would be permitted to describe deposits of strontium-90 in baby teeth for about the price of a large order McDonald's fries. Conversely, it would cost him approximately two new cooling towers if he were to publicly decry the possibility of some terrorist flying a plane into New York's Indian Point nuclear plant.

Predictably, the issue of patents on harrowing nuclear data has attracted its share of shrill First Amendment detractors. "It's my right as an American to talk about nuclear winter," asserted Muffy Wentworth, Sierra Club member and author of the book *Nuclear Winter: Sure Way to Beat Global Warming!*

The concept of nuclear winter—of global firestorms with gale-force winds, followed by interminable years of darkness and cold—is, like similarly inconceivable nuclear calamities, discounted by a growing body of market-driven data suggesting that, if it hasn't happened yet, it's never going to happen.

President Obama would be the first to agree.

PALESTINIANS IN AMERICA

AN INTELLIGENT SOCIALIST'S GUIDE TO TONY KUSHNER, WITH A KEY TO THE UN DECLARATION OF HUMAN RIGHTS[6]

Scene: an elevator, downstage right. Stuck inside are ROY COHN and ETHEL ROSENBERG, characters in Tony Kushner's landmark play, Angels in America. *McCarthyite lawyer ROY prosecuted Julius and Ethel Rosenberg, who were accused of spying for the USSR and executed in 1953. ETHEL now paces impatiently, pushing elevator buttons. Above the stage, recent* New York Times *headlines wink on and off didactically:*

"CUNY Blocks Honor for Tony Kushner," "Kushner, a Probing Dramatist of Intellectual Scope and Empathy," "In Reversal, City University Trustees Approve Honorary Degree for Tony Kushner."

ETHEL: So Tony, you want to tell us why you're writing this corny elevator skit? You thought maybe, "Ethel Rosenberg and Roy Cohn, trapped—how amusing"? This is a fakakta idea, Tony.

(Lights, upstage left, where TONY KUSHNER is at his desk, his back to us.)

ROY: Let the boy alone, Ethel. Don't you see he's got conflicts? You go back and help Julius assemble tractors in the dustbin of history.

ETHEL: Conflicts, Tony? You want I should advise you on the conflicts you probably got about that fancy new degree they're giving you at the City University of New York? The one you almost didn't get because Mr. Jeffrey S. Wiesenfeld of the board pointed out you criticized Israel? *(TONY crumples a page, tosses it over his shoulder.)*

ROY: Shut up, Ethel. It's good to stop Tony from dumping on Israel, so he can keep getting awards. That's great for me—I'm a bigger guy in Hell since they showed reruns of that *Angels* play of his on HBO.

ETHEL: Such nice goyishe actors they got to play us, Roy. But we must ask: Why did Tony criticize Israel?

Tony is a good boy. Tony does not exploit the masses. He criticized because he saw the Palestinians in pain and denied their rights. So Tony gets another degree, but inside he knows there are dialectically historical conditions that must be analyzed.

ROY: Thank you, Ethel, for validating my work in sending you to the electric chair. You were much less repulsive when you stole secrets of the A-bomb. Tony, I'm guessing you put me here to talk sense. So don't listen to this pinko puke. You got a good life—awards, honorary degrees. The people love Tony Kushner, who is, according to the *New York Times,* a dramatist of "empathy"![7]

ETHEL: Which is why Tony, as a feeling person, said that what was done to the Palestinian people when Israel was created was "ethnic cleansing." This is where Tony's analysis must continue—

ROY: Tony made a little mistake about the Palestinians. There weren't any. He assumed the native riffraff around in 1948 had feelings. Typical liberal moral-equivalence fallacy.

ETHEL: But this Mr. Wiesenfeld says Tony's an "extremist." He says his mother would have called Tony a "Nazi collaborator." *(TONY snaps a pencil in two.)* This is enough to alienate Tony from his means of production, Roy. *(TONY puts his head in his hands, groans.)*

ROY: *(Pointing to TONY)* Now, look what you did. Christ, Ethel, *never* remind Tony about those guys who call you a Nazi if you disagree with them. They can be scary.

ETHEL: Yeah. Like you were in the 1950s, when you called people Reds.

ROY: Tony, if you're going to force me to deal with this Bolshevik broad, I demand you write me with a cigar and some booze. *(Pause. ROY reaches into his coat pocket and fishes out a lit cigar and a glass of bourbon.)* Thanks.

ETHEL: Speaking of ethnic cleansing, Tony, did you read in the papers what happens to Palestinian protesters? How many Palestinians you think could be writing award-winning plays if they weren't being shot by the IDF?

ROY: Tony, *relax.* It's all good. Remember how your liberal supporters came through for you? Then you tell your detractors you always believed in Israel's right to exist—Fantastic! And, in case anyone notices, you're on the board of Jewish Voice for Peace, you say you're against the boycott—Nice save! It's like a built-in loyalty oath: "I am not now, nor have I ever been, a critic of Israel."

ETHEL: So Palestinians are supposed to stop suffering until Tony Kushner gets his honorary degree? All through this media mishegas, nobody talks about Palestinians—

ROY: Wrong! Wiesenfeld tells Jim Dwyer of the *Times* that Palestinians "worship death for their children" and "are not human."[8] So the liberals, in order to get the award back for Tony, have to act like Palestine doesn't exist—which ain't hard, 'cause it don't. After all, the whole point of the campaign is to defend Tony, not to help Palestinians, right?

ETHEL: You're a sick man, Roy.

ROY: No sicker than anybody else about this thing, Ethel. So Wiesenfeld gets props from the conservatives; Tony gets props from the liberals, and Israel gets props from everybody. It's a win-win-win situation!

ETHEL: Not for the Palestinians. Tony, you write about them! Put, for instance, a Palestinian in this script. You call yourself a socialist? You stand up, Mr. Socialist Writer!

ROY: World's a stage, Ethel. People love to play "commie," put on the T-shirts. Don't mean anybody's a goddamn radical about anything. It's all show biz.

(TONY stands up, kicks over a wastebasket. ETHEL crosses to ROY and pours the bourbon over his head. ROY starts to choke ETHEL. Suddenly, the stage shakes, and an ANGEL, played by KARL MARX, crashes through the backdrop and hovers over the stage. He speaks with the voice of a bored elevator operator.)

ANGEL MARX: Much as we'd all like this play to end happily, its material conditions do not permit divine intervention. So everybody out! Third floor: consumer goods, fetishized commodities, lingerie, light bulbs, bulldozers, hummus, hammers, sickles, yarmulkes, kafiyahs, flotillas, manifestos, bull horns, sirens, plasma, surgical supplies . . .

(Actors playing ROY and ETHEL shrug, step out of the elevator, and head back to the dressing room. TONY sighs, turns off his computer, and wanders off. Lights out.)

WHERE WILL ALL THE MUSLIMS GO?

OUR FUTURE FAHAD HASHMI AWARD[9]

NEW YORK – Every year about this time, since way back in 2010, the City of New York has bestowed its prestigious Hashmi Award upon a worthy New York resident who lives openly as an observant Muslim. The Hashmi recipient—preferably of Asian, Middle Eastern, or African descent—must have paid taxes, abided by Western law, held no criminal record, and valued higher education. Most of all he or she must have demonstrated all-around Good Muslim Sportsmanship in the war against terror.

The Hashmi, according to New York City's police commissioner, "is our way of saying, 'Thanks, observant Muslims, for allowing us to project our post-9-11 fear and hatred onto you. Your sinister hijabs, skullcaps, and beards, not to mention your wacky halal food, justified years of the NYPD secretly monitoring your communities. Although our Demographics Unit has been officially shut down, don't think we don't still notice you."

In a dignified ceremony at City Hall, the Hashmi honoree is presented with a pair of complimentary waterproof socks and a rain poncho. The lucky prizewinner is then immediately arrested on suspicion of intent to give these items to Al Qaeda.

The Awards Committee would again like to honor a deserving man or woman of the Islamic faith. Unfortunately, the Committee can't seem to find one. Virtually all New York's observant Muslims appear to have been deported or are assumed to be on the down-low, hoping to avoid "persecution."

The Hashmi Award was named for the ultimate Good Muslim Sport, Syed Fahad Hashmi. Mr. Hashmi, born 1980 in Pakistan, did not, unfortunately, begin life as a Good Sport. When he was three, he moved with his family to the United States and became an American citizen, thus succumbing to his inborn jihadist urge to infiltrate Western society.

The youthful Mr. Hashmi soon launched himself on a downward spiral, moving ever deeper into the netherworld of fanaticism by not smoking, not drinking, not cursing, respecting his teachers, pursuing an interest in current events, and abusing his First-Amendment rights in criticizing U.S. foreign policy.

By 2003, when he received a degree in political science from Brooklyn College, Mr. Hashmi had all but completed his descent into terror. Seeking to expand Islam's worldwide web, he went to England to study for a master's degree in international relations at the London Metropolitan University. There, Mr. Hashmi, in a wanton perversion of niceness, allowed an acquaintance, Mohammed Junaid Babar, to spend two weeks in his apartment. He also permitted Mr. Babar to use his cell phone and to stow some luggage. Luggage of doom, as it turned out: for it contained waterproof socks, raincoats, and ponchos that Mr. Babar allegedly later delivered to Al Qaeda in Pakistan.

Mr. Babar was arrested in 2004 and jailed. To avoid a prison sentence, he agreed to testify against the real terrorist: the vile, apartment-renting, guest-welcoming, sock-storing Syed Fahad Hashmi.

Mr. Hashmi, 26, was arrested in London in 2006, extradited to New York, and held in solitary confinement under Special Administrative Measures for three years before trial. Then, a miracle. In detention, cut off from family, friends, and most sensory stimuli—while contemplating a possible 70-year sentence—Mr. Hashmi allowed the healing power of Good Muslim Sportsmanship into his heart as his personal savior.

Finally embracing the tenets of Western Enlightenment, Mr. Hashmi made the inspiring decision to plead guilty to one count of providing material support to Al Qaeda. By so doing, he saved the U.S. government millions upon millions of dollars in the beefed-up security that would have been needed for news media to evoke the proper level of dread and revulsion.

Mr. Hashmi now resides in the Florence, Colorado ADX, the most locked-down prison in the United States, where he will probably spend every remaining day of his 15-year sentence. Unlike observant Christians serving time for bombing abortion clinics or murdering doctors, Mr. Hashmi lives alone in a bathroom-sized cell, devoid of human contact, where, as one reporter from the UK's *Guardian* put it, "The only possible means of communicating with other humans is to yell into the toilet bowl and hope that someone may hear."

All this, for non-Muslim New Yorkers, makes not having a Hashmi Award recipient especially hard to bear. "I'd hate to see that award disappear," said veteran gay rights activist Herbie Brownstein, in an impromptu sidewalk interview. "We of the LGBT community doff our chapeaux to Mr. Hashmi and to the other brave folk of Islam who, in this, and so many other legal cases, have taken the place of us commie fags as the main threat to civilization." Mr. Brownstein is president of the New York Chapter of Militant Communist Homosexuals for Domination of the Entire Globe.

"I hate that evil Muslim," interjected passerby Mildred Knucklewrapper, who teaches third grade in the Bronx. "Thanks to that guy, we may never know how many terrorists in South Waziristan now go to bed with dry feet. That Hashmi Award is the perfect way to remember why we need to forget about people like Syed Fahad Hashmi."

This reporter would have asked a challenging question at this juncture, but was afraid to be seen as supporting terrorism.

SEX SANS THE CITY

(A POST-MARXIST PREVIEW)

(Sex and the City ran on HBO from 1998 to 2004. What really eroticized the sitcom was all its brand-name, pillage-the-planet merch. Here is an episode that I translated for my Marxist-Leninist affinity group, so we may better throw off our Tiffany shackles.)

Scene I: *Chic, Upper West Side restaurant*

SAMANTHA: *(Striding in elegantly and sitting at table where the girls are waiting)* Greetings, comrades! How glad I am that I—sexy, fifty-year-old blonde girl, being fabulous and having much sex with men—meet you in favorite haute bourgeois bistro for sex talk. Look at dick-bulge of sultry, ethnic waiter—is not fabulous?

MIRANDA: *(Rummaging impatiently through briefcase)* Waiter dick unimportant for proper ordering, comrade. I, being caustic, hard-driven attorney with bright red hair, styled to evoke Great Mistakes in Hedge Trimming, not have time for frivolity. Must get back to office to shill for corporate capital—

SAMANTHA: Ooh, "shill"—sounds sexy, comrade!

MIRANDA: It is, comrade! Today, I defend sexy Fortune 500 company owning Indian Point—nuclear power plant making much electricity for city—from selfish, unsexy officials who warn of nuclear disaster. My logic: Why upset capitalist system?

CHARLOTTE: *(Sighing pertly)* For myself, comrades, I—token person of dark hair color—esteem the finding of Perfect Monogamous Soul Mate as most high goal in consumerist free-market society. This is exalted dream for which masses labor, regardless of increasing work hours, fear of layoff, dwindling surplus profit, endless war—and possible nuclear disaster. Heedless, heedless masses!

CARRIE: *(Flexing highly toned abs, set off to perfection by jaunty, $5,000 Christian Dior ensemble resembling clothes of Carmen Miranda after werewolf attack)* Ah, comrades— how good it is to exploit our lives in my column, earning many thousands of dollars more than other writers who, unlike me, have college vocabulary and knowledge of world history! *(She signals waiter)* Greetings, comrade bit actor of exotic descent who is destined to receive five dollars each time this episode is played in rerun! Please give us four of your most costly watercress omelets, removing yolk and other caloric nutrients. Hurry—before more radioactive groundwater leaches from Indian Point into Hudson River!

CHARLOTTE: Comrade! This is too much food! Is not anorexia the neoliberal pre-condition for true female happiness?

CARRIE: You are mistaken, comrade. We must order many expensive things—regardless of whether we shall actually consume them—so that our power may grow! Profit motive of late capitalism dictates terms of feminine value, and we must obey.

CHARLOTTE: Agreed.

MIRANDA: Carrie, I am loving of your shoes!

CARRIE: Shoes are foot-warping, spine-crippling Manolo Blahniks, costing $865! You see, comrades, glamorous allure of destructive footwear comes not only from physical sacrifice to wearer, but also from labor of anonymous, underpaid serfs who toil in abusive, outsourced factories. It is suffering of all classes that creates societal clout of Manolo Blahnik—name of brand you can trust!

ALL: *(Toasting)* Carrie is our leader! Long live vanguard of post-industrial alienation from means of production!

Scene II: *Carrie at home. Poised on her bed in the adolescent contortions of a twelve-year-old with a stamp collection, she types on her sleek MacBook Platinum, now available online for under $12,000.00. Her voiceover narration:*

CARRIE: Later that night, I wonder why virile mogul boyfriend, Mr. Beeg, refuse to commit. Could this mirror my own sublimation of need for basic human contact into acquisition of designer commodities? *(Close-up of glowing computer screen, as Carrie types:)* "Commodity fetishism: good or bad—and what if meltdown occur at Indian Point?" *(Suddenly, sirens blare; horrific explosion is heard)*

Scene III: *Back at stark ruins of Manhattan bistro; the stunned, disheveled four are staring, in bleak, Chekhovian fashion, into a dimming sun setting over the roiling Hudson.*

MIRANDA: Men are annoying.

CARRIE: Men are peegs.

SAMANTHA: I try lesbian sex. Too much talk.

CARRIE: Gay men better. Make good pets.

CHARLOTTE: I, with Jewish husband, for whom I

convert, have adopted child from faux-Communist country. Husband is kind; we are happy. Yet we never speak of Palestine.

MIRANDA: Please halt unsexy talk of Middle East, comrade.

SAMANTHA: Say, does anybody know why we are only four left alive after tragic—and totally unexpected—disaster at Indian Point?

CHARLOTTE: Perhaps something about Carrie's shoes?

CARRIE: Correct, comrade! Thanks to healing power of Manolo Blahniks—commodity onto which we magically project desire to survive—we are, for now, protected.

CHARLOTTE: *(Clutching stomach)* Comrades, I do not feel so good.

CARRIE: You must believe, comrade—believe in the brand.

MIRANDA: Must get her to shoe store, quick!

SAMANTHA: Ooh, "store"—sounds sexy, comrades . . .

(Holding one another up, they hobble off in search of Fifth Avenue.)

ANOTHER SAPPHIC RING CYCLE

Gay men think they know about opera. Ha. They don't know about *lesbian* opera, which, like lesbians themselves, is deeply misunderstood. I just happen to have a scenario for a grand opera by and for lesbians, absolutely chock-full of tragic splendor. *Regardez:*

ACT I

Naughty and heedless Clarinda, a baby dyke just out of reform school, arrives at the lesbian town of Uterville on the very day the locals are holding their joyous Festival of the Social Change

Workshops! Lesbian peasants and nobles alike, in brightly colored overalls and drawstring pants, sing and dance to their simple womyn's folk songs, while the naughty Clarinda goes around putting itching powder on everyone's sex toys.

Enter: Phollabia, Queen of the Lesbian Social Change Activists and Keynote Speaker. Stunned by Phollabia's beauty and momentarily paralyzed with infatuation, Clarinda sings the ever-popular aria "La Donna Immobile." At last, Clarinda gains an audience with the Queen by pretending that an evil therapist has turned her into a Republican male, and that only the kiss of a Lesbian Pure in Politics can break the curse. Phollabia, who can never resist a Cause, kisses the naughty and heedless Clarinda, and the two fall in love.

Suddenly the lights dim and all the oxygen is sucked out of the theater.

ACT II

Scene: U-Haul Rental office, holy site of the happy duo's Legal Same-Sex Wedding Ceremony. Nuptial music fills the hall as a retinue of swans smoking cigars escorts Clarinda, in nymph costume, to the altar. There Phollabia stands, dressed as Leon Trotsky. The lovers plight their troth, singing the majestic and politically aware "Coupletalist Duet."

"I was once a working-class Capitalist," recalls Clarinda.

"And I was once an upper-class Communist," replies Phollabia.

"But now," both sing, "we are as One: The People's Republic of Us!" And they take turns piercing each other's nostrils.

Comic relief is provided by a chorus of Celibates, who perform the piquant "Dance of the Test-Tube Babies." Villagers offer the couple an homage of toasters and microwave ovens, as Clarinda asks the musical question, "Is That All We Got?" A golden U-Haul arrives to take the newly committed pair . . . somewhere else.

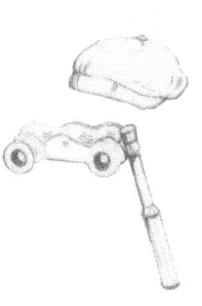

ACT THE THIRD

A year later.

Scene: A humdrum rent-stabilized cottage, deep in the forest. The naughty Clarinda feather-dusts the Certificate of Legal Same-Sex Marriage hanging on the wall while she awaits the arrival of her Activist Queen. In an attempt to spice up their relationship, Clarinda has donned a Bo Peep costume and sings of how wonderful it will be when her beloved returns home to act out the part of the sheep.

Enter, finally: Phollabia, exhausted from a hard day on the picket line. "What's for dinner?" she cries.

"How about some nice hot sex!" teases the naughty Clarinda, shaking her booty fecklessly in the face of her paramour.

"What?" gasps Phollabia. "Sleep with you while there remain states in our country that deny our people the legal right to wed? NEVER!" And she sings the magnificent aria, "Ne Me Touche Pas, I am Fighting Injustice."

To drown her out, Clarinda plays Goth love songs real loud on the radio.

That night in her dreams, Clarinda is visited by the Twelve Steps, each more hideous than the last. She wakes up and gets a cat.

ACT IV

Repeat Act III, but with more cats.

ACT V

At last, every region in the world has legalized same-sex marriage. This is the final blow to the couple's sex life. In deep mourning, they hold a huge, government-sanctioned renewal of their wedding vows but refuse to admit swans. The lonely and bereft Clarinda sneaks away from the crowd and sings: "Tis awful to be lawful; O Phollabia, why didst we not elopia?"

The residents of Uterville are unable to attend the wedding but send toasters instead. More and more toasters pile up onstage. A fight breaks out in the audience.

CURTAINS

SCIENCE PROVES AMERICANS ARE WORLD'S ONLY HUMANS[10]

NEW YORK – Recent evidence demonstrates beyond doubt, scientists say, that citizens of the United States alone possess the properties belonging to *Homo sapiens*. The discovery was announced today at the Center for Global Disaster, a Washington-based conservative think tank. Dr. Richard Shrapnel, head of the center, called the finding a paradigm shift. "Hell, I'd bet my opposable thumbs on it," he stated.

"Because of the enormous drain on the military budget, our research funding was cut," Dr. Shrapnel explained, "so we at the CGD were reduced to watching hours of old footage of the U.S.

invading Baghdad, sitting through endless reruns of *Homeland,* and reading the major tabloids. Over and over again, we saw Americans embodying dignity, worth, the ability to self-actualize through reason and will power—traits that comprise what we think of as human. Conversely, non-Americans—Arabs, for example—repeatedly appeared not to have these qualities. We were stumped. Then, one day, we looked at each other and realized we'd stumbled on the key to Western civilization: United States citizens are human beings! All the other nationalities are just people wannabes!"

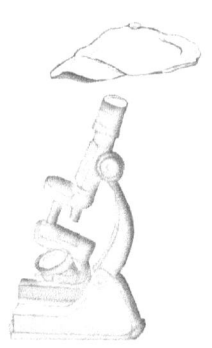

Researchers immediately set out to test their hypothesis by interviewing typical Americans on the street.

"For cryin' out loud," exclaimed Sy Plunderton, real estate broker and ex-Marine. "Any moron can see that Arabs aren't human. They keep dying; we keep not caring. What more proof you want? Sheesh, you eggheads take forever to figure things out."

Christine Detritus, marketing consultant, agrees. "I support our troops. They're human beings, for

God's sake. Not like those whining Iraqis who complain every time somebody bombs them and carry on like their homes are the World Trade Center or something. They just don't value human life the way we do."

Scholars predict this breakthrough will profoundly affect major academic disciplines, particularly the field of anthropology. "It could reconfigure the concept of evolution itself," surmises Dr. Joan Bloodloss, Senior Fellow at The American Homunculus Foundation. "Although we still believe our species began in Africa, we are now beginning to see that those individuals who migrated north and westward—particularly across the Atlantic Ocean—developed more advanced traits as they went, until they reached the North American continent, just below Canada and above Mexico, where they became full human beings.

Those who migrated in other directions have remained essentially bipedal primates. You'll see this pattern all across Europe, I believe—except for the French, who are, as usual, rapidly devolving. The Iraqis and Afghans? I'm not even sure if they're mammals. We won't really know until we can stuff some of them and put them in museums."

Psychiatry is also expected to undergo revolutionary changes in the wake of this study.

Psychotherapists continue to view their chief goal as instilling in their patients a healthy self-concept. However, a healthy self-concept for an American patient now appears to be an advanced state of megalomania.

Dr. Siegfried Schadenfreude, author of *I'm OK, You're in a Detention Camp,* observes, "The balanced, functional American sincerely believes that he or she alone matters, and is imbued with godlike powers over life on this planet. If you're merely self-centered and infantile, you're not going to make it in this world. For example, I had a homosexual man come to me, who was deeply troubled by all the things he'd done in Afghanistan as a soldier. But I convinced him that, since he couldn't justify the war on terror as a 'gay issue,' he needn't worry about it. Now, my client is as grandiose and fatuous as any U.S. president. It's living proof of how great this country is."

American news media endeavor to reflect just this sort of reality and, by all accounts, continue to do an excellent job of reporting the travails of U.S. and proto-human NATO troops stationed around the world. In the interest of maintaining total objectivity, however, American media seldom portray the damage and suffering incurred by whatever life form resides in, say, the Gaza Strip.

One of the news clips studied by the CGD, for instance, was a 2003 CNN report that allotted four minutes to an American airman with his arm in a sling, describing the difficulties his unit experiences outside Basra. It then cut to a soundless, .05-second clip of a screaming Iraqi toddler, his head covered with blood. One of the most objective news photos was the image of orange smoke blossoming over the city of Baghdad. "That's a town of almost 6 million people," said Lynn Oilrig, TV news anchor. "It's like we were bombing New York City—except, of course, that there are hardly any human beings in Baghdad."

Brigadier General Melvin Bottlerocket, military advisor to the U.S. Shadow Government, admitted that the situation in the Persian Gulf frequently upsets him. "I've had eyewitness reports of a 4-year-old Iraqi girl whose back was broken on the first night of shelling," he said. "Thousands of children, mothers, fathers, old people have been killed outright, their survivors dispossessed, abused, hurting. I feel awful. Then I turn on TV news and remember—Hey, that's how the West was won."

Chuckling in a humanitarian fashion, the general excused himself to go memorize a few xenophobic jokes to bolster officer morale.

PART 2:
A COUPLE OF
CLOSE-UPS

HERMAN AT HOGWARTS"

I t could be worse, I say to myself, as I buy my Trailways ticket, he could be on death row. He could be dying in a prison infirmary; he could be getting beaten up by racist gangs. Instead, Herman Bell is doing twenty-five years to life at a prison outside New York City, where we can take the bus to visit him and make sure he's OK.

It's Herman's birthday today, and my partner Laura and I are meeting our friends Tynan and Lise and their daughter Frankie, who have driven here from Montreal, to New York State's Eastern Correctional Facility.

Tynan is female-to-male transsexual; Lise is his partner. Laura and I met them almost ten years ago at Meow Mix, a punk-lesbo bar on New York's Lower East Side, where Laura spoke on a panel about her time in prison. The four of us are what the bohemian Zeitgeist would call "queer," though Frankie, a latecomer now approaching the terrible age of two, remains undecided. We're all part of a radical international undertow of free-market holdouts who believe there is such a thing as "political prisoners" in the United States and that, furthermore, they—after decades behind bars—should be let out. And because race matters, you'll need to know that we're white, and Herman, like a disproportionate number of his fellow prisoners, is Black. In fact, he's a former member of the Black Panther Party.

The five of us enter the huge grey building, which manages to achieve a look that's both looming and funky. Sort of like Satan's version of Harry Potter's Hogwarts, if Satan were clinically depressed. We go through the usual inane procedures of emptying pockets and taking off jackets, shoes, watches, earrings to get through the metal detector. Frankie, who looks like she could be packing a rod, is also searched. Afterwards, the guards stamp our hands with the "security" ink that can be recognized only by the prison's UV-reader, identifying us as visiting non-terrorists. Then they unbolt the door to the visiting room.

Inside is the usual fluorescently lit din. Dozens of parents and friends and wives and girlfriends, sitting in plastic chairs at Formica tables with men in dark-green prison suits, trying to make each moment count, as little kids yell and race each other to the vending machines. We find a table, buy bad, machine-dispensed coffee—and in comes Herman, a tall, sweet-smiling, quiet man—coach of the prison's football team. He leans down to hug us, one by one. Herman is fifty-eight years old today. He has spent the last thirty-three years in prison.

"GOOD!" scream headlines in New York City papers. "Don't Let This Killer Walk"; "Keep Bell on Ice." In front of news cameras, Patrick Lynch, president of the Patrolmen's Benevolent Association, declares, "These cold-blooded assassins and domestic terrorists should remain in jail for the rest of their lives."

Herman is a "model prisoner," who has earned two college degrees in sociology; he's started and participated in lots of programs mentoring other men in prison. He has maybe one chance in twenty of getting out when he comes up for parole again next month. The PBA wants to reduce that chance to zero.

In 1973, when he was in the Black Panther Party, Herman was arrested and charged, with Panthers Anthony (Jalil) Bottom and Albert Nuh Washington, in the 1971 shooting deaths of two New York City police officers, Joseph Piagentini and Waverly Jones. According to media accounts, Piagentini and Jones were responding to a domestic abuse complaint when they were killed on the streets of Harlem.

Diane Piagentini, Joseph's widow, appears on TV with Lynch to urge that Herman be denied parole "from now until the end of time." They flash an ugly mug shot of Herman in his Panther days, nostrils flared, eyes fierce in a "Get-Whitey" scowl. A monster.

Here, at the correctional facility, Herman cuddles the squirming Frankie, then lets her down to play. I watch Laura touch Herman's arm and ask him how's he's doing. Coming here is hard for Laura, who's done over fourteen years in prison herself. "After your arrest, the cops spend time harassing you and knocking you around," she told me once. "Then they take your picture, looking all miserable and mean, to scare people."

In court, Herman and his codefendants argued that they weren't guilty: that the FBI, under J. Edgar Hoover's Counterintelligence Program, cooked the evidence. The first trial ended in a hung jury; the second resulted in life sentences for the defendants and a book contract for the district attorney.[12]

"Understand—there was a war going on between police and the Black community," says Laura, who spent years in the Weather Underground, supporting the Panthers. I roll my eyes and wonder if there is ever not a "war going on" when tragic, stupid, needless deaths happen. Yet, after Herman's conviction, an ex-Panther witness came forth to say that his testimony against Herman was the result of police torture. Another war casualty.

I cannot judge Diane Piagentini. I don't know if I'd be able to stop hating, in her place. And yet, someone has.

Miraculously, someone has. Waverly Jones Jr., son of the other slain officer, has come to New York twice now, with some of his family, to ask the parole board to let Herman Bell out. Jones, a baby when his father was killed, has stated, "Nothing would give us more pleasure or joy than to see that man walk out of prison doors."

This is stunning, almost unprecedented. But, given America's predilection for Law and Order, "rot in jail" vengeance, which allows the condemned, even in the face of pleas from the likes of Desmond Tutu and the Pope, to be duly executed, this is not important. So we don't talk about this with Herman. We barely talk about parole.

Here in the visiting room, we've started a little birthday party. Pouring water into Coke bottle caps, we toast one another with pinkies extended, and gossip. Herman, with a plastic spoon, cuts a somewhat aged Reese's peanut butter "cake," and we sing Happy Birthday.

Herman wants to hear about Laura's and my cat, Rhoda, whose mission is to distribute orange fur evenly around the globe. Ty and Lise talk about working in the "Victory Garden" that Herman organized from prison, which once distributed fresh vegetables to inner cities. Herman chuckles at how bad the football team he's coaching is, but he's excited about his new granddaughter, Simone. He remembers back when he was in Mississippi, a sharecropper's kid, catching fish on the banks of a river after a rain. He seems like a kid again when he says, "We just had so much fun." Though his face looks suddenly crinkly and puzzled at the other memories that arrive.

Frankie is now intently exploring her overalls with another two-year-old, and I wonder what's happened to Herman here; how he gets through, as he's called it, "one more day on the plantation." But surviving evil doesn't make you a good person:

Surviving evil and not passing it on does. I've visited Herman for years now, and I would trust this good man with my life. Herman has actually saved lives in here . . .

But they've just announced visiting hours are over, and we gather up Frankie, who is not even a little tired. We turn to go, and Herman admires the beat-up leather jacket I've pulled on. I say, "Yeah, Laura got it for me. Sixteen bucks, streets of New York." Herman smiles, "Would you help me pick out one like that when I get out?"

What? What did he say? "When I get out"? Did you forget how you're hated, Herman? Am I supposed to say, "Be reasonable, go back to your cell now, go back to be strip-searched and monitored and controlled, but don't worry, Herman, we'll see you when we can, you know, there may be times when they won't let us in, but we'll keep trying to reach you through the vengeance and fear, we'll all grow old together, and we'll always hope. After all, Laura got out. Is that what I should tell you, my dear friend, my brother?"

I look up at him and I say, "Yes. Goddamn, yes. With all my heart, I would love to help you pick out that jacket, Herman. It would be an honor."

IN HANDCUFFS, SMILING

Once upon the 1980s, I was living an unremarkable life as a writer in New York City. Then I fell in love with a prisoner. Anyone will tell you that this is a really bad idea. It gets worse. I fell in love with a leftist lesbian prisoner who bombed the U.S. Capitol.

She, along with two men and three other women, were political prisoners because they did what they did to protest U.S. government policy. They called their case the Resistance Conspiracy case and were facing multiple decades behind bars for a series of property bombings that targeted various government and police power bastions. The basis for the defendants' high-profile status with the Feds was, of course, the fact that they had chosen the Capitol Building to bomb in protest of "our" invasion of Grenada and shelling of Lebanon.

Having come from the depraved wholesomeness that was the Midwest in the mid-twentieth century, I had somehow made it to New York City in 1982. Along the way I became a feminist and came out as a lesbian. Due to the unhappiness embedded in my lower-middle-class origins, I nurtured a perennial suspicion of money and power. So when I heard about these Resistance Conspiracy case characters, I was intrigued.

The sites that the group was accused of bombing were, from my point of view, fairly well chosen symbols of power. They included the Patrolmen's Benevolent Association after the 1984 police shooting of African-American grandmother, Eleanor Bumpurs, and the apartheid-era South African Consulate, along with our friend, the Capitol Building. No one was killed or injured in any of the blasts. The Capitol's Republican Cloak Room was damaged, and Teddy Roosevelt's bust busted. Small injuries, compared to the overthrow of a sovereign country.

The indicted prisoners, I noticed, were educated, middle-class, white people. "What the hell were they thinking?" the wholesome, Midwest part of me wondered. Didn't they know they were throwing away their lives? Wasn't taking up arms a tactical disaster, almost sure to hurt the

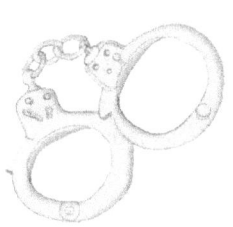 innocent while giving the government another incentive to upgrade its firepower?

Yes.

But.

Given the delusion of a viable democracy in this country, anything that broke the anesthetic grip fostered by such minions of "fairness and balance" as National Public Radio was a relief.

I agreed with them; I disagreed with them. I needed to know who they were. A feminist newspaper hired me to write a story on the four women in the case. I read attorneys' briefs and defendants' political pamphlets. I studied photos of the accused. They all seemed non-insane, intelligent people, yet because of their antigovernment stance, they had drawn inordinate, record-breakingly long sentences from previous charges.

Susan Rosenberg, for instance, was already carrying a sentence of fifty-eight years for explosives possession. Linda Evans had incurred forty-five years for giving a false ID to purchase three legal guns. Then there was Laura Whitehorn, unconvicted, who at that point had spent more time in jail—almost four years—without bail than any prisoner in U.S. history. I looked at Laura's photo. She was wearing a kafiyah and smiling with a sort of luminous determination, her fist in the air. "She looks so bossy," I thought.

I went to Washington, DC to interview the four women.

The DC Jail was noise and grime and a brutal hopelessness, permeated by squawking, indecipherable PA announcements, fluorescent lighting and the omnipresence of guards, or "corrections officers." The COs, most of whom were Black, looked bored and often hostile, and seemed to carry around a sense of shame to be working there. The prisoners—95 percent African American—wore jumpsuits, usually rumpled and too big or too small.

Then, one by one, the unusual white women were led into the glass-walled cubicle, where I waited to interview them. Susan Rosenberg was first. I asked her questions about the case; just what, I don't remember. She answered them and was taken away. Marilyn Buck was brought in next, then Linda Evans. They each talked reasonably, candidly, about their political views, the years inside they were facing, how those years didn't matter, given the power they were fighting. Yet the picture I was getting seemed diffuse, incomplete.

Finally a small, grey-haired woman with deep brown eyes was led in, in handcuffs, carrying a stack of legal papers. She grinned and offered me a roll of the "Silence = Death" stickers that ACT UP was then cranking out to fight HIV/AIDS. As Laura Whitehorn answered my questions, I realized that this case was beginning to come into focus for me. She was able to combine complex layers of fact with a gut-level identification with suffering. I was also startled to find that I was quietly, perversely, becoming happy. Several hours later, on the train home to New York, I figured out that I had a large crush on Laura Whitehorn.

I was euphoric and deeply shocked, after we exchanged a few letters and cards, when the feeling became mutual. Soon, we realized we loved each other. Laura's bail never happened, but a plea bargain did. Laura was finally sentenced—the maximum of twenty-three years—and she was transferred to the Lexington, Kentucky women's prison.

So began for me years of the low-grade terror that comes with loving someone who is in constant danger. In prison, Laura, like her codefendants, had virtually relinquished the "white skin privilege" that allows most Caucasians to be treated as human beings. Like her Black and Latina friends in the general prison population, she could be beaten up, or put in "the hole," for various infractions. Like other political prisoners, Laura could at any time legally be confined to a sensory deprivation unit. She could die of bad medical care. Once, on a summer afternoon in the first year of our love, I fell asleep and dreamed that I was moving, flying through a blackness to reach the someone I loved the most. Such lift, such hope: Only to find myself face to face with a skull.

Then there were our political fights. How could I be in this relationship without signing on as a Revolutionary? Why did I criticize armed struggle?

"I would die for my principles," Laura said during one of our arguments.

"And I would die for my right to remain ambivalent," I retorted.

We talked on the phone, but only when Laura called me; as you probably know, it's impossible to call a prisoner. We visited, but only when I had the money to go to Kentucky; later, California. I must have seemed to her cloying and demanding, always wanting to talk about "feelings." Our conversations were suffused with misunderstanding, longing, anger. Always, they were monitored by guards or federal agents.

I hated myself for being "codependent" enough to love a prisoner. After all, this relationship appeared, according to the wisdom of the Self-Help industry, to be a textbook example of codependency. I wondered if I was crazy. Friends and therapists and psychics told me in one way or another: This is hurting you too much. She's using you. Let her go. She would want you to be happy.

Laura herself told me to see other people. But how could I, when I loved her so much? I couldn't. I tried. I failed miserably. To the unsuspecting world, I must have acted weird and self-involved. I must have treated friends badly. Certainly, I lost friends.

Finally—you knew it was coming, didn't you?—Laura and I did the sensible thing. We broke up. Me on the outside, Laura in prison; we went on with our lives.

Not. We couldn't really go on with our lives. Inevitably, stupidly, masochistically, wonderfully: we got back together. And in August 1999, after fourteen years and three months of incarceration, Laura Whitehorn, having served her time, walked out of prison.

Not that the advice wasn't sound; not that my friends didn't care; not that I don't still think she can be bossy, or that we don't still fight about politics. But all these years later, Laura and I are together and, last time I checked (about a second ago), we plan to be for the rest of our lives.

Here's the payoff. No matter how life-canceling a prison wall is, life can slip through. I would have known Laura anywhere. She just happened to come to me in handcuffs, smiling. She is the only person in the world who has meant the sun to me. I will spend the rest of my life being grateful and happy that she is out.

Because so many similar stories don't end this way, I want to dedicate this one to anyone who's loved impossibly. To anyone who continues to love through death and disease and difference and distance and all the impenetrable barricades—including prison— that life can put up. And to the women and men behind bars whom I know or have yet to know, please hang on. Love is as tangible as the body, you know, regardless of where our bodies are.

AFTERWORD

LAUGHING LIFE, DANGEROUSLY

When I was a kid, my dad tells me, I boasted about my family—all of Eastern European Jewish ancestry—in the following way: "I have two grandmothers. One is Jewish and the other lives in Kansas." It was around that time that I shushed a prominent religious studies scholar, a friend of my father's, for saying "Jesus Christ." "That's a bad word," I reported to my parents, pleased with what remained of my prudent good nature.

Years later, when I was in high school, I wrote a column in the student newspaper mocking Santa Claus as a bigot who only visits chimney-endowed homes to deliver his war-toy wares produced by exploited children. It was, like many of my best ideas, highly derivative of jokes I learned from years of reading *Calvin and Hobbes* and *Bloom County* comic strips. The column, admittedly, was sophomoric—which is embarrassing since I was, at that point, a junior.

The response, however, was scandalous; in the heavily Jewish area of South Florida in which I lived, the article generated some Jew-hating commentary from some Santa-loving Christians. A group of people surrounded me at lunchtime, threatening me great bodily harm. The informal mob's leader accomplished a syntactical victory when he called me a "dirty Jew racist."

The principal responded by sending me home to protect my safety. My hatred of injustice was rankled by her inability to take a strong stand against racism and humorlessness. My hatred of school was sated by the unexpected long weekend.

Yet my attempts to silence Jesus Christ or expose Santa Claus pale in comparison to the delicious scoops Susie Day reveals to us here. Santa Claus to head the NSA? I hope he doesn't remember my article. Jesus to resign his post as lord and savior in favor of a clean garage and the great human novel? Maybe he's not such a bad word after all.

This is a book of dangerous revelations. Between the terror of the Wealthy Underground Organization and the war on terror, the responsibility of the artist and the dissident, Susie Day revels in danger. In Susie Day we have a real original: a muckraking satirist. Equal parts Jessica Mitford and John Waters, with just a dash of Joan Rivers, Susie Day helps us laugh in and through struggle. Who else could wade into the Orwellian world of permanent war and counterrevolution with a smile?

Who else could focus our attention on prisons and homophobia and police brutality and wealth disparity and popular culture to show that these damnable institutions can also be, with the right person at the keyboard, damn funny?

There are real scoops here, and not just the ones involving disgraced politicians or the secret-life-of-revolutionary-kitsch. (Poor Che Guevara; how was he to know that his belief that the actions of a few could spark the actions of the many had in fact been a driving belief of capitalism since a cabal of European landowners decided a few hundred years ago that all those serfs needed to pay rent on the land they were forced to work?) The news from Snidelandia concerns the merger of the well-known and the barely known elements of power.

In a brilliant, dense, and not-at-all-funny book, *Scenes of Subjection,* scholar Saidiya Hartman offers a stunning accounting of slavery. Its power, Hartman tells us, lay not just or even primarily in the spectacle of abused and mutilated bodies. Rather, the fundamental power of slavery was in the "mundane and quotidian" expressions of power that Hartman excavates across a variety of settings.

In a most different register, *Snidelines* accomplishes a similar feat: Susie Day gives us an accounting of the contemporary world by examining its mundane and quotidian abuses. Through playful, scathing, renderings of all-too-many police murders of Black men, upward wealth redistribution, homophobic violence, and the legal dead zones that have swallowed up increasing numbers of Muslim communities—some well known, others not at all—Day provides a power map of the sad state of affairs in which we now find ourselves. (As an aside, it seems to me that a subtext of many of these essays might just be the inadequacy of our contemporary discourse: "Islamophobia" and "homophobia" seem poor descriptors of the particular oppressions they name; any word whose root can also be applied to an aversion of spiders might not be the best way of conceptualizing such intricate forms of domination.)

My career as a satirist was short-lived. Not only did I recoil from the unexpected danger of the job, but I also realized that I lacked the necessary chutzpah to pull it off. The long hours, the faux interviews with financiers, superheroes, and homosexuals, the dedicated attention to the dystopic events of the day with a flair for imagining humorous parallel universes; it just was not my style. Instead, I traded it in for the relative ease of writing people's history about left-wing social movements and prison politics. I decided to spend years on end visiting numerous archives and interviewing dozens of revolutionaries (including Day's ne'er-do-well spousal equivalent, Laura Whitehorn).

I couldn't figure out how to make people laugh at power, at least not in any original or meaningful way. So I turned my sights to those who have tried to fight power in a variety of ways. (Did you know that there was once a clandestine group with a name eerily similar to the Wealthy Underground Organization? Look it up, you'll see. The only question is: which Bob Dylan song did these Wealthy terrorists take as their inspiration? And why doesn't anyone ask about their role in the alleged destruction of the Left?)

However, reading Susie's words—piecemeal as they come over the electronic transom, or collectively as they are assembled in this book—I am forced almost to platitudes of the "laughter is the best medicine" variety. A joke a day will dismantle empire, abolish prisons, and generate an antiracist, queer-feminist, socialist society? Well, maybe not, though it certainly couldn't hurt.

This, too, is something I appreciate about Susie's work: *Snidelines* prompts us to laugh at ourselves more. It is not just Them who oppress us that can elicit a pained laugh at the state of the world.

It is also Us, as Day hilariously and rather brilliantly reminds us in essays like "Palestinians in America," in which one of the most brilliant conceits of twentieth-century theater, the imagined conversation between martyred communist Ethel Rosenberg and the villainous prosecutor who pursued her murder, Roy Cohn, that punctuates Tony Kushner's *Angels in America* is revived to critique Kushner's weak-kneed response to critique from right-wing Zionists in 2011. This one-act play powerfully imagines the role of the artist in wartime, amid critique, by extending that dialogue between Rosenberg and Cohn. You can almost hear the Yiddish seeping through the pages as these archenemies, a sweet communist and a vile reactionary, debate art and politics while we the readers are asked to recommit to the high standards a political life requires. Not bad for a girl from Kansas City.

Hell is other people, Sartre told us long ago. The Left may not be hell—maybe; the people's tribunal is still deliberating on that one—but we are funny. And not just telling jokes funny, but stodgy and stumbling funny. And we need to be able to laugh at our foibles and follies. Day does us one better, helping us laugh at them by amplifying the absurdity, by mixing Our tactics with Their politics in order to rethink both.

In the end, *Snidelines* evinces the greatest, most subversive danger of all: love. As her cats, friends, and partner of more than twenty-five years can all attest, Susie Day is not just a satirist but a sentimentalist. Her quick wit and sharp tongue are still powered by a loving heart. I knew this when I sat down to read *Snidelines,* and yet I still found myself tearing up at the beautiful final essay, a tribute to love—both the love of her life and the transformative power of love itself. A reminder that the best satire is a catalyst, not a distraction, love is the perfect note on which to conclude this tome. The essay gives us all the opportunity to glimpse, a TMZ-worthy inside-look at, the relationship between Susie Day and one Laura Whitehorn. And in doing that it rewards us with the insight that love is tangible and meaningful and worth something. It makes us human, despite and because of and notwithstanding all the other terrible things that make us human and less-than-human. It is not that love in the abstract conquers all or always wins. But it is love in the daily relationships and actions we take, maybe not love for The People but certainly love for people, abstractly and specifically, that makes us better than all that would deny us our potential humanity.

Surviving evil and not passing it on makes you a good person, she tells us in her poignant essay about longtime political prisoner Herman Bell. I'm not sure if skewering evil and passing on the joke makes one automatically a good person, although it is clearly part of what makes Susie Day such a good person.

I can't wait to see who will play her in the movie version.

Dan Berger
May Day 2014, Seattle

ENDNOTES:
A BIT OF BACKSTORY

Defense Secretary's Bullet Slays
Brooklyn Youth

[1] Timothy Stansbury Jr., 19, was unarmed and trying to get from one building to another to attend a birthday party in the Louis Armstrong housing project, Bedford-Stuyvesant, Brooklyn. Opening the door to his building's roof, Stansbury was shot by Officer Richard S. Neri Jr., who was patrolling the project, and died within minutes. Officer Neri was suspended for thirty days without pay and his gun was taken away. (Robert D. McFadden and Ian Urbina, "Fatal Shooting Not Justified, The Police Say," *New York Times,* January 25, 2004.) (Daryl Khan, "Officer in 2004 Fatal Shooting Is Given a 30-Day Suspension," *New York Times,* December 31, 2006.)

[2] Jim Harper, "You're Eight Times More Likely to be Killed by a Police Officer Than a Terrorist," CATO Institute website, August 10, 2012 (http://www.cato.org/blog/youre-eight-times-more-likely-be-killed police officer-terrorist), citing Washingtonsblog.com, June 21, 2011: "Fear of Terror Makes People Stupid" (http://www.washingtonsblog.com/2011/06/fear-of-terror-makes-people-stupid.html).

Terror by the Wealthy Underground

[3] In 2009, stockbroker Bernard Madoff pled guilty to eleven federal felonies for defrauding thousands of investors (many of them actual people)

of billions of dollars. He is scheduled to be released from prison in 2139.

Former Weather Underground member Laura Whitehorn made occasional tax-free contributions to this piece.

No Way in My Manger

[4] Regarding "that idiot in Congress" who made the comment about "legitimate rape":

In August 2012, Representative Todd Akin (R-MO), asked in an interview whether abortion is justified in cases of rape, said, "It seems to be, first of all, from what I understand from doctors, it's really rare. If it's a legitimate rape, the female body has ways to try to shut the whole thing down." John Eligon and Michael Schwirtz, "Senate Candidate Provokes Ire With 'Legitimate Rape' Comment," *New York Times,* August 19, 2012.

Jesus Quits as Evangelical Savior

[5] Scott Lively, *The Pink Swastika* (Springfield, Mass., Veritas Aeterna: 2002). Also found online. Enjoyable extracts include: "[W]e have accumulated a substantial amount of new documentation supporting our thesis that the Nazi Party was conceived, organized and controlled throughout its short history by masculine-oriented male homosexuals who hid their sexual proclivities from the public . . ." http://www.thepinkswastika.com

PALESTINIANS IN AMERICA

[6] Early in 2011, the City University of New York voted to deny an honorary degree to *Angels in America* playwright Tony Kushner because CUNY trustee Jeffrey S. Wiesenfeld alleged Kushner had criticized the state of Israel. Thus began a heated public debate, more about Kushner's right to the award than about the neglected rights of Palestinians, which had been the reason for Kushner's criticism of Israel in the first place. In a *Democracy Now!* interview lasting almost an hour on May 10, 2011, Kushner managed to mention Palestinians only once. CUNY finally allowed Kushner to claim his degree, so this story is officially over. But awards like this don't help Palestinians much; furthermore, collecting awards shouldn't eclipse an artist's expression of the truth.

[7] Ben Brantley, "Critic's Notebook; Tony Kushner, a Probing Dramatist of Intellectual Scope and Empathy," *New York Times,* May 7, 2011.

[8] "I tried to ask a question about . . . vigorously debated aspects of Middle East politics, like the survival of Israel and the rights of the Palestinians, and which side was more callous toward human life, and who was most protective of it.

"But Mr. Wiesenfeld interrupted and said the question was offensive because 'the comparison sets up a moral equivalence.'

"Equivalence between what and what? 'Between the Palestinians and Israelis,' he said. 'People who worship death for their children are not human.'

"Did he mean the Palestinians were not human? 'They have developed a culture which is unprecedented in human history,' he said."

Jim Dwyer, "A University Trustee Expands on His View of What Is Offensive," *New York Times,* May 5, 2011.

OUR FUTURE HASHMI AWARD

[9] In 2004, Fahad Hashmi, an American citizen, allowed an acquaintance to use his cell phone, briefly stay with him and store nonmilitary supplies, allegedly for Al Qaeda, in his London apartment. For this, he was sentenced in 2010 to serve fifteen years for supporting terrorism. At the time of this writing he remains in solitary confinement at the US "supermax" prison in Florence, Colorado. Many Muslim-Americans have similar cases. (See the website, no-separate-justice.org)

SCIENCE PROVES AMERICANS ARE WORLD'S ONLY HUMANS

[10] By the time this book appears, what began as the war on Iraq may have morphed into World War VII. The empirical fact that so many U.S. citizens have remained silent, expressing no concern or grief for the deaths of millions of foreign individuals caused by our government would appear to confirm the continuing validity of this scientific discovery.

HERMAN AT HOGWARTS

[11] At the time of this writing, Herman Bell is still incarcerated, though he's been transferred three or four times to other prisons. Herman is now sixty-six years old and held at the Great Meadow Correctional Facility in Comstock, NY. He has come before the New York State Division of Parole six times—four more times since I wrote this—and denied each time, due to the "nature of the offense." He is scheduled to appear again early in 2016.

[12] Robert K. Tanenbaum, *Badge of the Assassin* (New York: Simon & Schuster, 1979); later, a made-for-TV movie.

ACKNOWLEDGMENTS

This book would have been nonexistent without the encouragement and support of a lot of wonderful people (and a couple of cats who, to avoid over-cuteness, shall remain nameless). You'd think that dedicating this book to her would be enough, but no, I must again thank Laura J. Whitehorn, the best thing that Karma ever did for (or to) me. It probably took more faith and resolve for Laura not to let me give in to existential dread about this project than it took her to get through fourteen years of prison.

Indestructible props to Valentina DuBasky, whose dedication to her own visual art has inspired me for years. Valentina and her esposa Andrea Piccolo started Abingdon Square Publishing and encouraged me to put this book together.

Voluminous gratitude to Diane Samuels, playwright, author, teacher, whose friendship and abiding belief in the human spirit have guided and supported me for a couple of decades, now.

Deep respect to Alison Bechdel, whose presence, from 1983 on, has taught me focus, faith, and a stoic belief in "the work itself."

A raised fist in salute to Bill Ayers, whose kind spirit and generous editorial advice were revolutionary in shaping this book.

To the people who encouraged me to do this book, or encouraged me in general, not unlike: Barbara Zeller, Tim Murphy, Scott Tucker, Dan Berger, Dana Barnett, Tynan Jarrett, Franca Jarrett, Harriet Clark, Suzy Subways, Mark Sullivan, Cheris Kramarae: Thank you.

I thank my lifelong friend Randy Thomas. He always gets mad at me when I neglect to tell him I've published something, so we should all keep this book a secret from him.

Finally, gratitude to *Monthly Review* and my job there. Saludos, comrades.

BIOS

Susie Day, writer

Susie Day would be a household name if she had decided to call herself "Flashlight." She was born a long time ago in Springfield, Missouri, but endured most of her childhood traumas in Kansas City.  She now writes, attends rad-lib demonstrations, and has a day job in New York City, where she lives with her much cuter and more politically radical partner, Laura Whitehorn.

Maria Pia Marrella, illustrator

 Maria Pia Marrella is a painter, designer, and illustrator who lives in the Hudson Valley region of New York. She found Day's thought-provoking essays inspiring in creating the illustrations for this book.

Author photograph by Camilo Godoy
Illustrator photograph by John Cisternino

www.ingramcontent.com/pod-product-compliance
Lightning Source LLC
Chambersburg PA
CBHW071944170626
46813CB00005B/1822